45 4074576 X

D1390606

Introduction

A: Legal and management

B: Health and welfare

C: General safety

D: High risk activities

E: Environment

Contents

Introduction

Overview

The purpose of this book is to explain the basic health, safety and environmental steps that you, your employer and the site or project that you are working on should be taking.

The content gives easy to understand information and practical guidance. Each chapter starts with a summary of what sites and employers should do for you, as well as what they expect from you.

It has been written to assist operatives and specialists sitting the CITB *Health, safety and environment test*, which is an important requirement when obtaining a construction industry scheme card. The card gives proof that individuals working on construction sites have the required training and qualifications.

The content follows the *Health, safety and environment test* structure.

GE 707 is also the official supporting document for the CITB Site Safety Plus one-day *Health and safety awareness course*.

Feedback

If you have any comments on the content, suggestions for improvement or extra topics your feedback would be welcome. You can contact us by email or telephone as outlined below.

 publications@citb.co.uk

 0344 994 4122.

Acknowledgements

CITB wishes to acknowledge the assistance offered by the following organisations in the preparation of this edition of GE 707.

- ☑ Construction Plant-hire Association
- ☑ Environment Agency
- ☑ Institute of Demolition Engineers (Vernon Watson)
- ☑ JRC Associates Ltd
- ☑ JSP Ltd
- ☑ Lendlease
- ☑ Norse Energy Ltd
- ☑ Simian Risk Management Ltd
- ☑ Thames Laboratories
- ☑ Willmott Dixon

Work-related injuries and ill health statistics for the construction industry

- [✓] Approximately 2.65 million people are employed in the UK construction industry. It covers activities including housing, utilities, repair and maintenance, refurbishment, demolition, roofing, shopfitting, mechanical and electrical, plumbing and highways maintenance.

- [✓] The UK construction industry is made up of about 194,000 construction businesses, of which 90% employ fewer than 10 workers.

- [✓] On average 43 construction workers are killed each year due to accidents. In 2014-15 there were 35 fatal injuries to workers (20% lower than the five year average). There were also four fatal injuries sustained by members of the public.

- [✓] In the last five years 217 workers have died in the construction industry.

- [✓] The biggest killer (around half) is falls from height, with an average of seven people dying each year as a result of falling through fragile roofs.

- [✓] In 2014-15 there were 1,833 specified injuries (such as falls from height, or slips, trips and falls on the same level) and 3,581 over seven-day injuries.

- [✓] The most common over seven-day injuries are due to manual handling/lifting accidents (30%), slips, trips and falls on the same level (21%), falls from height (11%) and being struck by an object (11%).

- [✓] The health and safety statistics for 2014-15 show there were 69,000 cases of work-related ill health. Around 40% of these were new conditions, that had started during the year, and the remainder were long-standing conditions. Of the 69,000 cases, 45,000 were cases of musculoskeletal disorders, 14,000 were cases of stress, depression or anxiety and 10,000 were cases of other illness (such as skin or respiratory conditions).

- [✓] In 2014-15 an estimated 1.7 million working days were lost; 1.2 million due to ill health and 500,000 due to workplace injury, making a total of 0.8 days lost per worker.

- [✓] The construction industry has the largest burden of occupational cancer. Over 40% of occupational cancer deaths and registrations involved people who worked in construction.

- [✓] The most significant carcinogen is past exposure to asbestos, followed by silica, solar radiation, and coals, tars and pitches.

- [✓] Approximately 5,000 people die each year due to past exposure to asbestos.

- [✓] Work-related respiratory disease covers a range of illnesses that are caused or made worse by breathing in hazardous substances (such as construction dust) that damage the lungs.

- [✓] In 2005 it was estimated that 600 people died from silica-related lung diseases (caused by dust from cutting blocks, kerbs, and so on). Many more suffer from occupational asthma or are forced to leave the industry due to work-related ill health.

- [✓] Vibration white finger, carpal tunnel syndrome, occupational deafness and dermatitis are the most common non-lung diseases suffered by those in the construction industry.

 Construction workers (just like you) could die due to work-related ill health, or as a result of an accident, if control measures are not followed.

A message from the Health and Safety Executive

There have been big improvements over recent years in reducing the number and rate of injuries to construction workers. Despite this, construction remains a high-risk industry and accounts for a high percentage of fatal and major injuries.

What is less recognised is that construction is a high-risk industry for health issues too.

Every year more working days are lost due to work-related illness compared to injuries. The statistics reveal that construction workers have a high risk of developing diseases from a number of health issues. Construction has the largest burden of occupational cancer amongst the industrial sectors.

Anyone responsible for putting people to work on a construction site must ensure they have obtained, or are in the process of obtaining, the necessary skills, knowledge, training and experience to carry out the job or task in hand. Being competent is not the same as simply being trained to do a job.

Workers can play a vital role in improving health and safety standards on site. By contributing to the consultation process with both their employer and principal contractor, they can help to prevent dangerous conditions from developing on site. Workers need to develop their skills in identifying risks and be confident in speaking out when they notice that something is wrong.

This *Safe start* publication will help construction workers understand some key points about the risks they face, why the risks are significant and what they and their employers need to do to manage these risks to remain healthy and safe.

This publication will also serve as a reference source for the *Health, safety and environment test* as well as the supporting course material for the CITB Site Safety Plus one-day *Health and safety awareness (HSA) course.*

Attending a site induction

Setting out

Construction is an exciting industry. It is constantly changing as projects move on and jobs get done. As a result of this, a building site, without the proper management systems and controls, could be a dangerous environment to work in. But accidents and ill health can be avoided if everyone on site works together.

A free online film, *Setting out*, explains what you and everyone on site must do to stay healthy and safe at work.

This film is essential viewing for everyone involved in construction, and should be viewed before you sit the CITB *Health, safety and environment test*. The content of the film is summarised here, and these principles form the basis for the case studies in the test.

Part 1: What you should expect from the construction industry

Your site and your employer should be doing all they can to keep you and your colleagues safe.

Before any work begins the site management team will have been planning and preparing the site for your arrival. It is their job to ensure that you can do your job safely and efficiently.

Five things the site you are working on must do are listed below.

☑ Know when you are on site (signing in and out).

☑ Give you a site induction.

☑ Give you site specific information.

☑ Consult with you on matters which affect your health, safety and welfare.

☑ Keep you up to date and informed.

Part 2: What the industry expects of you

Once the work begins, it is up to everyone to take responsibility for carrying out the plan safely.

This means you should follow the rules and guidelines as well as being alert to all the changes on site.

Five things you must do are listed below.

☑ Respect and follow the site rules.

☑ Safely prepare each task.

☑ Complete each task responsibly.

☑ Know when to stop (if you think anything is unsafe).

☑ Keep learning.

Every day the work we do improves the world around us. It is time for us to work together to build an industry that puts its people first. By working together we can build a better industry that respects those who work in it.

Working well together

The Working Well Together (WWT) campaign is an industry-led initiative that helps micro and small businesses improve their health and safety performance. The campaign's activities include health and safety awareness days, designer awareness days, breakfast and evening events, roadshows and regional WWT groups.

"EVERY WEEK ONE OF US DIES"

 To find out how the WWT campaign can help you and your company, go to wwt.uk.com

How to use GE 707

GE 707 follows the standard structure that is used across all core CITB publications.

Section A: Legal and management

Section B: Health and welfare

Section C: General safety

Section D: High risk activities

Section E: Environment

Section F: Specialist activities

Each chapter begins with a summary list of what your site and employer should do, together with a corresponding checklist that explains what you should do for your site and employer.

Use of icons

A set of icons stresses important points within the text and also directs you to further information. The icons are explained below.

 Website/further info   Important   Case study

 Example   Good practice   Quote

 Question   Poor practice   Definition

 Ideas   Caution   Checklist

 Notes   Consultation   Video

 Favourite   Guidance

Augmented reality

Augmented reality (AR) technology is used in our publications to provide readers with additional digital content such as videos, images and web-links.

This technology has been used to connect you with extra and complementary content. This can be accessed via your mobile device when you install the Layar app.

Simply download the 'Layar' app and use the camera on your smartphone or tablet to scan an appropriate page.

 How to install the app

☑ Go to the appropriate app store (Apple or Android) and download the Layar app (free of charge) to your mobile phone or tablet.

☑ Look out for the AR logo, which indicates that you are on a Layar-friendly page.

☑ Open the Layar app and scan the Layar-friendly page (ensure that you have the whole page in view whilst scanning).

☑ Wait for the page to activate on your device.

☑ Touch one of the buttons that have appeared to access additional content.

Where can I find augmented reality in this publication?

The table below identifies the pages in this publication that are compatible with augmented reality and the information that can be accessed when an active page is scanned.

Page	Content
Cover	Watch a product demonstration
	Buy related products
5	Watch the *Setting out* film
204	Access the training record

Glossary

Many words and terms that you will hear on a construction site are explained in the main part of this book. The list below includes some more terms that you might come across.

Adhesive. A substance used for sticking things together.

Abrasive wheel machine. A machine, such as a bench-mounted grinder or a disc-cutter, which is used for cutting or grinding materials.

Allergy. A damaging reaction of the body caused by contact with a particular substance.

Asbestos. A naturally occurring, heat-resistant substance that was once used extensively in construction work. Breathing in asbestos particles is harmful to the lungs.

Asthma. An illness that causes difficulty in breathing.

Bacteria. Germs that can cause some illnesses.

Barrier cream. A protective cream applied to your hands before starting work.

Bracing. Scaffold poles that make a scaffold rigid.

Brick-guard. A metal mesh fitted to a scaffold to prevent anything from falling through the gaps between the guard-rails and toe-board.

Cable ramp. A temporary 'hump' laid over a trailing cable to protect it from damage by people or traffic passing over it.

CCTV. Closed circuit television.

CDM. Construction (Design and Management) Regulations.

Cherry picker. A type of MEWP on which a passenger-carrying basket is located on the end of an articulating or extending arm.

Consultation. The action or process of formally consulting or discussing (for example, a manager asking you for your input whilst carrying out a risk assessment).

Control measure. Putting measures in place to reduce the risk to an acceptable level (for example, guarding on a machine).

COSHH. Control of Substances Hazardous to Health Regulations.

Crush injuries. Injuries caused by something crushing a part of the body.

Distribution system (electrical). The method that is used to get electrical supplies to where they are needed on site.

Double-handling. Having to move something twice.

Edge protection. A framework of scaffold poles and scaffold boards erected around a sloping roof to stop anything falling over the edge.

Employee. Someone who works for someone else.

Employer. Someone who has people working for him or her.

HAVS. Hand-arm vibration syndrome.

Hazard. Anything that has the potential to cause harm (ill health, injury or damage).

Health and Safety at Work Act 1974. The main piece of health and safety law.

HFL. Highly flammable liquids.

HSE. Health and Safety Executive.

HSE inspector. An official who can inspect the site and take action if work is not being carried out safely.

Lanyard. A length of fabric that connects a safety harness with a fixed strong-point.

Ligament. A band of tough body tissue that connects bones or cartilage.

LPG. Liquefied petroleum gas.

Method statement. A step by step description of how to carry out a job safely.

MEWP. Mobile elevating work platform.

PAT. Portable appliance testing.

PPE. Personal protective equipment.

RCD. Residual current device.

Risk. The likelihood of an event occurring from a hazard.

Risk assessment. A document identifying the hazards, risks and control measures for a particular activity.

RPE. Respiratory protective equipment.

Scissor lift. A type of MEWP with a platform that rises vertically.

Slewing. A part of an item of plant (such as the jib and counter-weight of a crane), rotating about a vertical axis.

Solvent. Chemical used to dissolve or dilute other substances.

Tripping hazard. Items lying around that you might trip over.

Ventilated. Supplied with fresh air.

Introduction

01
General responsibilities

A
01

What your site and employer should do for you

1. Provide a safe place to work.

2. Provide a safe method of work and safe equipment.

3. Eliminate or avoid risks where possible.

4. Tell you about the hazards and how the risks will be controlled.

5. Provide training and information so you can do your job safely.

6. Communicate with you and allow you to have your say.

What you should do for your site and employer

1. Go to and take part in safety inductions and briefings.

2. Follow the site rules and your safe system of work.

3. Avoid taking short cuts or risks.

4. Report anything which you think is unsafe.

5. Co-operate and get involved.

Introduction

Everyone on a construction site has a responsibility for health and safety, both morally and legally.

By knowing what is needed, you will be able to understand what you and your employer's legal duties are to protect your safety and health while at work.

A
01

This chapter will help you understand the following.

☑ What the law requires everyone to do.

☑ That employers must provide places of work that are safe for everyone.

☑ That safe systems of work must be planned and put in place.

☑ That the people involved need to be competent and trained.

☑ That communication has to be effective so everyone knows what is expected.

☑ That the Health and Safety Executive (HSE) can enforce the law.

 Competence

A combination of a person's training, skills, experience and knowledge and their ability to apply these to carry out a task safely. Other factors (such as attitude and physical ability) can also affect someone's competence.

What the law requires

The Health and Safety at Work Act 1974 was introduced to protect the health and safety of everyone at work.

Your employer is responsible for the following.

☑ Providing a safe and healthy place to work.

☑ Making sure you can work safely.

☑ Issuing tools, plant and equipment that are safe to use.

☑ Making sure that you are suitably trained and adequately supervised.

☑ Communicating information and instructions effectively.

It also means **you** have a **legal duty** to comply with your employer in all matters of health and safety.

A health and safety law poster must be displayed on every site. The poster outlines what you and your employer need to do.

 If your employer cannot display the health and safety law poster (for example, if you are a mobile worker) they should give you a card or leaflet that contains the same information.

Providing safe ways of working

The law requires employers to develop safe systems of work (a defined method of carrying out each job in a safe way).

The following documents can form part of a safe system of work.

- ☑ Health and safety policy.
- ☑ Method statements.
- ☑ Risk assessments.
- ☑ Permit to work.
- ☑ Construction phase plan.
- ☑ Survey results.
- ☑ Health surveillance.

Health and safety policy

Your employer's policy will give you the following information.

- ☑ Show you how health and safety is managed in your company.
- ☑ Identify what the arrangements are (how and what should be done).
- ☑ Show who is responsible for what (including **you**).

Method statements explain how the job is to be done safely. They will also identify the following.

- ☑ Materials and equipment to be used.
- ☑ People and skills needed.
- ☑ Sequence, method and controls to be followed.

Risk assessments explain the following.

- ☑ Hazards of the job (for example an open excavation).
- ☑ The significant risks (for example people falling in).
- ☑ Controls needed to minimise the risk to an acceptable level (for example erect a double handrail around all sides of an excavation) and requirements for PPE.

Your employer should assess the risks to both you **and** others arising from your work.

A *hazard* is anything that could harm you (such as chemicals, working from a ladder, or electricity).

The *risk* is the chance (likelihood) that you could be harmed by the hazard and how serious any harm could be.

Permit to work

- ☑ A system for controlling activities that are deemed high risk or need extra controls, (such as hot-work permits, permits to dig and confined space entry permits).
- ☑ A permit has strict controls and limitations which must be followed.
- ☑ You must never start any job for which a permit is needed before the permit's start time and before the permit controls are in place.

A **construction phase plan** is required for every construction project and must be regularly reviewed and added to as new trades start. It will give you the following information.

☑ Describe how the work has been safely planned.

☑ Explain how people will work safely together.

☑ Show how the site will be organised.

☑ Identify the main dangers on site and how they will be controlled.

Survey results

There are a number of surveys (for example, an asbestos, noise or COSHH survey) that may be required. The results of these surveys will form part of the safe system of work.

Health surveillance allows for ill health to be identified early. It is needed if you are exposed to a hazardous agent or if your work may have an adverse effect on your body (for example, hearing damage if you are working in a noisy area). It lets your employer check that their control measures are working and that you are not exposed to any ill health that could be prevented.

? Do you follow a safe system of work?

Are you familiar with your safe system of work? Do you know what the sequence of work is? Are you aware of the hazards? Do you have the right equipment and training?

Do you fully understand the identified control measures? Or are you doing it the way you have always done the job, the way you think it should be done or just having to make do with what you have got?

If you are working differently from the safe system of work written down then speak to your supervisor or employer. Your way may be better, quicker or more efficient but it may have other risks that your employer hasn't thought about. These will need to be assessed and if necessary extra controls can then be put in place.

People need to be trained

The law needs you to have the neccessary **skills**, **training**, **knowledge** and **experience** to carry out the tasks given to you. You should never be put in a position where you need to carry out a job for which you do not have the necessary requirements.

If you feel you are, then you may be putting yourself or others at risk – you need to speak to your supervisor or the site manager.

Sharing information and knowledge

Good communication of health and safety information is essential for everyone.

Employers have a legal duty to consult with their workforce. To be effective it needs to be two way (listen to as well as talk to).

A
01

This can be done in a variety of ways.

- [✓] Site inductions.
- [✓] Toolbox talks.
- [✓] Safety briefings.
- [✓] Worker involvement schemes.
- [✓] Informal chats/open door policies.
- [✓] Posters.
- [✓] Suggestion boxes.

Site induction

You must go to a site induction for each new site that you visit. As a minimum you should be told about the following.

- [✓] The site rules.
- [✓] Traffic management systems.
- [✓] Permits to work.
- [✓] Welfare facilities.
- [✓] Emergency and first-aid arrangements.
- [✓] PPE requirements.
- [✓] Environmental considerations and requirements.
- [✓] Areas of the site where you can and cannot go.
- [✓] The site hazards (for example, overhead power lines).
- [✓] How you will be consulted regarding health and safety matters.

Toolbox talks

These are short health and safety briefing sessions on a particular subject connected to the work being carried out.

The person delivering the toolbox talk should give you the opportunity to ask questions or raise concerns.

> **The aim of a toolbox talk is to give and share information to help keep you safe and protect your health.**

Worker involvement

Workers are often the best people to understand the risks in their workplace. Talking to, listening and co-operating with each other can help in the following ways.

- [✓] Identify joint solutions to problems.
- [✓] Raise standards.
- [✓] Reduce accidents and ill health.
- [✓] Help you and your workmates to do your job.

You may be asked to take part in a site inspection or audit and discuss your usual work methods. This will help your employer understand any problems you are experiencing and propose solutions.

 Have your say

Sites run suggestion schemes, regular safety forum/meetings and open door policies.

Please get involved – your views are important and can make a difference.

A
01

How the Health and Safety Executive enforces the law

The Health and Safety Executive (HSE) is a Government body responsible for overseeing most aspects of workplace health and safety in the UK. The HSE's main roles are listed below.

☑ Offer advice on workplace health and safety.

☑ Carry out workplace inspections.

☑ Conduct serious accident investigations.

☑ Carry out enforcement action for health and safety breaches.

The HSE has the following powers.

HSE inspectors can issue notices if they think it necessary

☑ The legal power to demand entry to the workplace without notice.

☑ Can interview you under caution.

☑ Can prosecute a company, an employer or an individual employee.

☑ Can issue improvement or prohibition notices that must be complied with.

☑ Can charge a fee for intervention.

Improvement notices

These are issued if something is unsafe, not up to standard or not being adequately controlled. They will say how the law was being broken and give a date by which things must be put right or improved.

Prohibition notices

These are issued when something is so unsafe all work connected to it must **stop** immediately. Work must **not** start again until the matter has been put right.

Fee for intervention

The HSE can charge an hourly rate for the time the HSE inspector spends investigating a breach of the law, including visits, letter writing and ensuring that the matter has been put right.

A
01

02

Accident reporting and recording

A 02

What your site and employer should do for you

1. Listen, and make sure any concerns you have are acted on.

2. Put measures in place that allow different trades to work safely together.

3. Encourage accidents, ill health and near misses to be reported.

4. Provide an accident book and make sure records are kept.

5. Make sure accident investigations are carried out, to understand what went wrong so they can be prevented from happening again (not to find someone to blame).

What you should do for your site and employer

1. Understand and follow your safe system of work.

2. Stop and take advice if you cannot follow your safe system of work.

3. Report any accident you have and enter it into the accident book.

4. Report any near misses or anything you think could be unsafe.

5. Co-operate with any investigation.

Introduction

 On average 43 construction workers are killed each year due to accidents.

The biggest cause of fatalities is falls from height.

In 2014-15 there were 1,833 specified injuries (such as falls from height, or slips, trips and falls on the same level) and 3,581 over seven-day injuries.

A
02

Year after year the same types of accidents and incidents are repeated.

Common types of accident and incident

☑ Falling from height.

☑ Slips, trips and falls on the same level.

☑ Manual handling.

☑ Being struck by mobile plant.

☑ Contact with electricity.

☑ Contact with moving machinery.

☑ Being trapped by something collapsing.

In many cases these could have been avoided by taking simple precautionary measures (for example, clearing up your work area regularly to reduce the likelihood of slips, trips and falls).

Prevention – what you can do

☑ Make sure you fully understand the safe system of work.

☑ Work to the instructions you are given.

☑ Follow the site rules.

☑ Do not be tempted to take risky short cuts.

☑ Keep your work and storage areas tidy (good housekeeping).

☑ Keep access routes and walkways clear of materials and equipment.

☑ Report anything you think may be unsafe to your supervisor.

All accidents and incidents should be reported. Your employer can then determine the cause and prevent them from happening again.

 Everyone on site has a responsibility to report unsafe conditions.

Accidents

You must make sure that any accident or injury you have is reported and recorded in the accident book.

A
02

Unsafe conditions

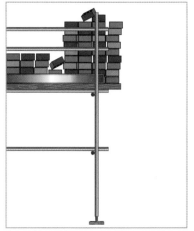

Something with the potential to cause harm

The following details **must** be recorded in the accident book.

☑ The injured person's name and address.

☑ The injured person's occupation.

☑ Date and time of the accident.

☑ Where the accident happened.

☑ How the accident happened.

☑ The injury that was sustained.

☑ Details of the person filling in the book (if different from the injured person).

Your employer must keep accident book information secure, as it is confidential.

If you witness an accident it is important you tell your supervisor or employer.

By reporting accidents lessons can be learnt that may prevent them from happening again.

More serious accidents and those that result in more than seven days off work have to be reported by your employer to the HSE.

Near misses

An incident that nearly resulted in an injury or damage

Accidents

An incident that causes physical injury

Unfortunately, not enough near misses or unsafe conditions are reported.

You may think reporting them will get you into trouble – but the opposite is true.

☑ Each one is a learning event.

☑ Reporting them can help to prevent accidents from happening in the future.

A
02

Occupational diseases

You must tell your employer if you develop signs or symptoms of the following diseases, or if a medical professional tells you that you are suffering from one of them.

☑ Hand-arm vibration syndrome, for example from using hand-held vibrating tools.

☑ Cramp in the hand or forearm.

☑ Carpal tunnel syndrome from vibrating or percussive tools.

☑ Occupational dermatitis (which, for example, you can get from working with cement).

☑ Occupational asthma from breathing in construction dust.

☑ Tendonitis or tenosynvitis in the hand or forearm, for example from repetitive or frequent movement.

☑ Occupational cancer, for example from exposure to asbestos or silica dust.

☑ Disease caused by exposure to a biological agent, for example leptospirosis (Weil's disease).

A
02

03

Health and welfare

What your site and employer should do for you

1. Identify work activities that could damage your health.

2. Tell you about the hazards and how the risks should be controlled.

3. Provide safe methods and equipment to minimise any exposure.

4. Provide you with free personal protective equipment (PPE), if required.

5. Provide good, clean welfare facilities.

B
03

What you should do for your site and employer

1. Understand how the hazards can damage your health.

2. Follow the relevant safe system of work.

3. Wear your personal protective equipment (PPE).

4. Do not misuse the welfare facilities and help keep them clean and tidy.

5. Ask if in any doubt and report any changes in your health.

Introduction

Work-related ill health has devastating consequences for individuals and their families but it is misunderstood and underestimated.

This is because the effects of exposure to most work-related ill health hazards are not always immediate (unlike an accident which causes injury). You may go home from work feeling more or less the same each day and are unaware of the effects.

As you are repeatedly exposed to small doses of dust, fumes or certain substances, exposed to loud noise or use a vibrating tool a lot, they start to damage your body. It can take many weeks, months or even years before symptoms of exposure become a problem to you and irreversible damage may well have occurred.

B
03

Common causes of work-related ill health

Noise and vibration

Refer to Chapter B08 for information on noise and vibration.

Respiratory (breathing) diseases

Refer to Chapter B07 for information on respiratory diseases.

Skin conditions

Dermatitis

This is a skin condition that is generally caused by exposure to chemicals and other harmful substances. Hands and forearms are most affected. It can be painful and will affect your personal life as well as your work life.

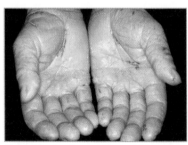

Dermatitis showing crusting and thickening of skin

Some of the symptoms are shown below.

☑ Redness.

☑ Itching.

☑ Dryness.

☑ Cracking or blistering.

The most common cause of dermatitis in the construction industry is working with cement. Wet cement can also cause burns.

Allergic dermatitis can make your skin so sensitive you will not be able to use some substances again, which could end your career.

Skin cancer

The number of skin cancer cases continues to increase every year. Those who work outdoors are at greater risk.

The following actions will help to prevent overexposure.

☑ Covering up by wearing suitable loose clothing and a hat.

☑ Using sun block on exposed arms, face and neck.

It is vital that you drink plenty of water to prevent dehydration.

 If you notice new moles or changes to existing moles seek medical advice as soon as possible. Don't ignore it – early treatment is vital.

Although less common, skin cancer can be caused by contact with mineral oils. Daily contact with items (such as oily clothing or gloves) can lead to a form of skin cancer. Mineral oils are common on mechanical plant and pipe threading machines.

Diseases carried in the blood

Leptospirosis (Weil's disease)

☑ This disease is carried by **rats** or **dairy cattle**. It enters the bloodstream through cuts and grazes.

☑ It is a particular problem when working on or near water, sewage, waterlogged sites or rat infested areas.

You can minimise the risks by taking the following precautions.

☑ Wearing suitable gloves.

☑ Keeping all cuts and grazes covered with a waterproof plaster.

☑ Washing your hands before eating or smoking.

Wherever possible discourage rats from coming onto site by putting all food waste in covered bins.

 The early symptoms are often like influenza (flu). If left untreated the disease may lead to kidney problems and can be fatal.

Tetanus (lockjaw)

☑ This is a disease of the nervous system.

☑ It enters the body through cuts, grazes or puncture wounds.

☑ Germs are found in contaminated soils or manure.

☑ An early symptom is an increasing difficulty in opening the mouth or jaw.

Hepatitis

☑ Hepatitis is usually caught from contact with infected needles and syringes.

- If you find any suspected drug taking equipment leave it alone and contact your supervisor or employer.

Legionella

This is a form of pneumonia, which can be caught in the following ways.

☑ From bacteria found in warm, damp places (such as air conditioning/hot water systems and cooling towers).

☑ By breathing in contaminated water vapour/mist.

A safe system of work is needed if legionella is suspected.

B
03

 If you think you may be suffering from hepatitis, tetanus or legionella, speak to your supervisor straight away and get medical advice.

Stress and mental health at work

Stress is the adverse reaction people have to too much pressure or other demands placed upon them. It is not an illness in itself, but can lead to you not being able to perform at work and have an impact on your health and wellbeing. Stress can lead to common mental health problems (such as anxiety and depression) and also physical chronic health conditions (such as heart disease, back pain, headaches, gastrointestinal disturbances and alcohol and drug dependency).

Work-related stress and common mental health conditions are closely linked with similar signs and symptoms. For people with mental health conditions, work-related stress can also trigger or worsen an existing mental health condition. Your employer should identify any signs of mental health conditions as early as possible so appropriate support and treatment can be given quickly.

The following actions may help to improve your mental health.

☑ Talk to a family member, a trusted friend or colleague or someone independent. Talking about how you feel is not a sign of weakness and having someone listen to you can often make you feel better.

☑ Look after your physical health. Good mental health is directly linked to good physical health. Physical activity, sleep and diet can all impact on your mental health.

☑ Do things that you enjoy (for example, a hobby, reading, sport) and try to avoid things that you don't.

☑ Recognise your limits, as this will help you recognise the things that are likely to have a negative impact on your mental health.

 Other sources of help are available. For further information refer to organisations such as Mind (www.mind.org.uk) and Time to change (www.time-to-change.org.uk).

Drugs and alcohol

Anyone caught working under the influence of illegal drugs, legal highs or alcohol will have to leave site immediately and could lose their job.

Many employers and clients have policies to carry out random testing for drugs and alcohol.

Prescribed drugs

☑ Over-the-counter and prescription drugs can have side effects.

☑ You should read the label or speak to the pharmacist if in doubt.

☑ Some hay fever medicines can make you drowsy, which could mean you are not safe to be on a construction site or fit to drive.

Illegal drugs

People under the influence of illegal drugs are a danger to themselves and everyone else on site. They are likely to suffer from the following.

☑ Poor or irrational decision making.

☑ Slow reaction times.

☑ Clumsiness.

☑ Distorted vision.

The effects and traces of some drugs can stay in your system for prolonged periods (for example cannabis can be detected during testing several weeks or even months after it has been taken). Unlike alcohol, there are no permitted safe levels for illegal drugs so a trace could mean failing a drugs test.

Legal highs

Legal highs are substances that produce the same, or similar, effects as drugs like cocaine and ecstasy, but are not controlled. It is illegal for them to be advertised, bought and sold as fit for human consumption. Drugs sold as a legal high may contain one or more substances that are illegal to possess.

 Just because a drug is legal doesn't mean that it is safe.

Legal highs can still cause harm and have similar health risks (for example, paranoia, seizures, coma and death) to illegal drugs.

Alcohol

Depending upon your employer or site policy the blood alcohol level needed to pass a test can be less than the legal driving limit.

Besides being a danger to themselves and others, anyone still under the influence of alcohol at work risks losing their job and livelihood. Of those people convicted of drink driving, many were driving the morning after a few drinks the night before. Most underestimate the length of time it takes to sober up.

B
03

e.g. **The effects of alcohol can last for hours**

On average it takes one hour for your body to get rid of one unit of alcohol.

A unit is the volume (litres) x ABV (% strength).

- ☑ One pint of 5% beer is 2.8 units.
- ☑ Five pints of 5% beer is 14.2 units.
- ☑ One 175 ml glass of 12% wine is 2.1 units.
- ☑ One 25 ml shot of 40% spirit is 1 unit.
- ☑ One 275 ml bottle of 5% alcopop is 1.4 units.

If starting at 7 pm and drinking five pints it could be up to 10 am the next morning before all the alcohol is out of your system.

B
03

Welfare facilities

Your employer has a legal duty to provide adequate welfare facilities, such as those listed below.

- ☑ An adequate number of toilets, separate for men and women (where this isn't possible, toilet doors should be lockable and separate from urinals).
- ☑ Toilet paper.
- ☑ Sanitary disposal facilities for women.
- ☑ Hand-washing facilities.
- ☑ Changing and drying rooms where necessary.
- ☑ Somewhere to take breaks from work.
- ☑ Chairs with back support (not canteen benches).
- ☑ A supply of clean drinking water.
- ☑ A means of boiling water for drinks.
- ☑ A facility to warm up food (for example a microwave).
- ☑ A means to secure valuables and change of clothes (for example lockers).

 The same welfare facilities must be provided for transient (mobile) workers.

Hand-washing facilities (not the canteen sink) must include the following.

☑ A supply of running hot (or warm) and cold water.

☑ Soap or hand cleaner.

☑ A way of hygienically drying your hands.

Welfare facilities must be kept clean and in good order. If they are not, then speak to your supervisor or the person responsible.

Site canteen area for taking breaks

 Welfare facilities are provided for your benefit – please look after them.

B
03

04

First aid and emergency procedures

What your site and employer should do for you

1. Tell you the first aid and emergency procedures during the site induction.

2. Display emergency information, contacts and telephone numbers.

3. Provide emergency and rescue equipment.

4. Provide first aiders and develop first-aid procedures.

5. Maintain emergency escape routes and equipment.

B
04

What you should do for your site and employer

1. Know how to raise the alarm.

2. Know what to do in an emergency or site evacuation.

3. Be aware of the emergency procedures relating to your own safe system of work.

4. Know where and how to get first aid.

5. Know where to gather if there is an emergency.

Introduction

Every site should have procedures in place in case of an emergency, such as those listed below.

☑ Fire.

☑ Collapse.

☑ People trapped or needing rescue.

☑ Serious injury.

☑ Chemical spill.

You must know the following information.

☑ How to raise the alarm.

☑ What the alarm sounds or looks like.

☑ The safe method or route of escape/evacuation.

☑ Where to go.

Information should be given during site induction and displayed on noticeboards or signs.

Remember – sites are constantly changing and so can emergency escape routes.

> **❗ Make sure you always know where your escape routes (and any equipment you may need) are.**

You should also be familiar with any emergency procedures that form part of your safe system of work (such as confined space entry and rescue from height).

First aid

During your site induction the following information should be explained.

☑ Who the first aider and/or appointed person is.

☑ How to find, contact or recognise them (for example green hat or sticker on hard hat).

☑ Where to get first aid treatment.

☑ Where to find the first-aid kit.

First-aid post

The aim of first aid is to reduce the effects of an injury, whether or not the injury was caused by the work itself.

Discovering a casualty

What you can do

If you are first on the scene of an accident your actions could be crucial.

You should do the following.

- ☑ **Make sure you do not put yourself in danger.**
- ☑ Assess the situation.
- ☑ If it is safe to do so remove or isolate the hazard.
- ☑ Go to the casualty and find out what's wrong.
- ☑ **Call for help** – if no-one comes go and find help and call the emergency services.
- ☑ Return and stay with the casualty until help arrives.

 It is crucial that time is not wasted. The priority is getting help (first aider) and the emergency services to the injured person as soon as possible.

What employers must provide

Accidents and injuries do happen on site and employers must provide the following.

- ☑ Trained people (such as first aiders) to respond to an incident, which takes into account shift work or holidays.
- ☑ The correct type of first-aid equipment for the hazards (for example, eyewash and burns kits).
- ☑ Arrangements for lone workers or when the first aider is not there a means to summon an ambulance or other professional help, for example an on site doctor or nurse.

They should also take into account how far the site is from a hospital or the emergency services.

First aid roles

An employer, based on the findings of their first aid needs assessment, could choose to appoint one or more of the following three roles.

- ☑ **Appointed person** – is appointed when a first aider is not needed in the workplace. They do not have to have training but they will look after the first-aid equipment and facilities and call the emergency services if needed.
- ☑ **Emergency first aider** – trained to give emergency first aid at work (EFAW) to someone who is injured or becomes ill.
- ☑ **First aider** – trained in first aid at work (FAW) and able to provide first aid for a greater range of injuries and illnesses to someone who is injured at work. Sometimes there may be other hazards on site, for example working in confined spaces; therefore extra training may be needed.

 If the first-aid box is empty you must inform the first aider.

05

Personal protective equipment

What your site and employer should do for you

1. Identify risks and eliminate them where possible.

2. Where there is still a risk, personal protective equipment (PPE) which protects you from those risks must be provided.

3. Supply PPE free of charge.

4. Provide facilities to clean, store and maintain PPE.

5. Show you how to correctly wear and care for your PPE, and where it should be worn.

B
05

What you should do for your site and employer

1. Wear your PPE at all times when needed.

2. Wear the right PPE for the task.

3. Put it on and adjust it so it fits correctly.

4. Look after your PPE.

5. Report any PPE defects.

Introduction

Personal protective equipment (PPE) consists of items and clothing designed to protect you from a variety of hazards. The type of PPE that is designed to protect you from respiratory (breathing) hazards, such as the inhalation of dust and fumes, is called respiratory protective equipment (RPE).

Your employer must ensure the following.

☑ A risk assessment is carried out to identify any hazards and risks, and what can be done to eliminate or control them.

☑ You are supplied with PPE whenever there is a hazard that cannot be eliminated or minimised to a safe level.

☑ You are supplied with PPE free of charge.

B
05

 PPE should only be used as a last resort.

Policies and site rules

Some sites have mandatory PPE policies or rules, which include the use of gloves and eye protection. This is because you can be exposed to a variety of hazards and risks, which can change daily and can be outside the control of you or your employer.

On most sites you can only take off PPE when you are in a safe area (such as the site office or welfare compound).

Wearing a combination of PPE

Some common examples of PPE are listed below.

☑ Safety helmets (hard hats).

☑ Safety footwear/boots.

☑ High-visibility clothing.

☑ Safety glasses (low-impact eye protection).

☑ Gloves.

There are times when you will need to wear other extra PPE, as identified in the following circumstances.

☑ By a risk assessment or method statement.

☑ Instructions from your supervisor or employer.

☑ From site rules/site induction.

☑ From signs and notices.

Other task-specific PPE is listed below.

☑ High-impact eye protection (for example, when using a disc cutter).

☑ Ear defenders (muffs) and earplugs.

☑ Safety harnesses and lanyards.

☑ Knee pads and overalls.

☑ Wet weather clothing.

☑ Lifejackets or buoyancy aids.

Task-specific RPE includes the following.

☑ Half or full face respirators.

Your employer must provide PPE, but you must be responsible.

☑ Take care of your PPE (keep it clean and inspect it regularly).

☑ Use your PPE as instructed.

☑ Stop work and report any lost or damaged PPE to your supervisor.

☒ **Do not** work without it where it is needed.

Types of personal protective equipment

Head protection

Safety helmets must be worn at all times, except when you are in a safe area.

A safety helmet is worn to protect you from falling objects or bumping your head. Your safety helmet will be most effective when you follow the guidelines below.

☑ Wear it the right way round (peak at the front).

☑ Adjust it so it fits snug and square on your head.

☑ Make sure it is fitted with a chin strap if there is a risk of it falling off while working.

☑ Make sure it is fitted with a proprietary liner for cold weather (not wearing it over your woolly hat).

Do not cut, drill holes, paint or apply unauthorised stickers to your safety helmet, as this can severely reduce its capacity to protect you in an incident.

Safety helmet to help protect against head injury

Do not wear hoodies or beanies under your hard hat. If extra comfort is needed to keep you warm an approved manufacturer's lining should be used.

Dropping your safety helmet from height onto a hard surface can also reduce the strength, even if there is no obvious damage. If this happens it should be replaced.

B
05

Foot protection

Safety footwear must be worn at all times on site and have protective toe-caps.

☑ Some types have a steel mid-sole to protect from puncture injuries (standing on a nail).

☑ Some offer better ankle support.

☑ Some offer good grip on slippery surfaces (such as safety trainers).

☑ Some offer increased comfort and are more suitable to trades (such as floor layers) who repeatedly kneel and bend their feet.

High-visibility clothing

☑ All staff and visitors on site should wear a high-visibility vest or coat as a minimum.

☑ There are three classes of high-visibility clothing.
- Class 1 – low visibility suitable for general sites.
- Class 2 – medium visibility needed when working on or near A and B class roads or heavily trafficked sites.
- Class 3 – high visibility needed when working on or near dual carriageways, motorways, airports or railways (same reflective strips as Class 2 but with long sleeves).

B
05

Body protection

Protective clothing can be used to protect against the following.

☑ Strong oils and chemicals (for example, cement).

☑ Fire hazards.

☑ Rough or sharp surfaces.

☑ Extreme cold or heat.

☑ Weather.

Hearing protection

There are two main types of hearing protection.

☑ Ear defenders or earmuffs.
- These have to be a snug fit to be effective.

☑ Earplugs.
- Make sure your earplugs are inserted properly.
- If they feel loose or fall out then they are not inserted correctly.
- Do not reuse disposable earplugs, as this can cause infection.

Eye and face protection

The three main types are shown below.

*Safety glasses
(low-impact eye
protection)*

Safety goggles

Face shield

Safety glasses and other forms of low-impact eye protection are not designed for tasks where high-impact eye protection should be worn (such as when using cartridge tools, grinders or disc cutters).

☑ Different types of eye protection protect you against the following.

- Flying debris and objects.
- Chemical splashes.
- Airborne dust.
- Molten metal and sparks.

☑ Eye protection needs to be regularly cleaned and stored to protect from scratching.

☑ You need to be able to see through your eye protection for you to be able to work safely.

☑ If your eye protection is scratched or keeps misting up then you need a suitable replacement.

 Safety glasses are only classed as low-impact eye protection and will not withstand an impact from flying debris when using grinders, disc cutters, cartridge tools, and so on.

Hand and skin protection

☑ Gloves should be suitable for the hazards and task. Using the correct type of gloves will protect your hands.

☑ If using chemicals the gloves should be impervious (the chemical should not be absorbed by the glove and inside onto your hands).

☑ It is important that gloves are regularly cleaned or replaced.

Barrier creams are no substitute for gloves but can offer an extra line of protection. Using hand soap, hand cleaners and after work creams to replace oils lost from your skin will help in prevention.

Never use solvents or spirits to clean your hands. These strip the protective oils from your hands leaving you more prone to attack. 5%-10% of construction workers working with cement, mortar and concrete are affected by dermatitis.

Flotation equipment, including lifejackets

☑ If you have to work near or over water where there is a risk of drowning, you should be provided with a buoyancy aid (such as a lifejacket). Wear it at all times.

☑ Falling in while wearing your work clothing and boots, and even tool belts will drag you under or sap your energy quickly, especially in cold water.

☑ Self-inflating lifejackets automatically inflate and turn you onto your back if you fall in, even if you are unconscious, allowing you to breathe.

☑ Other, more basic but equally important equipment (such as life-buoys, life-rings or throwing lines) may also be provided.

☑ Where strong currents or fast flowing water are present there may be a need for other equipment (such as manned rescue boats).

B
05

Types of respiratory protective equipment

To prevent exposure to harmful dust, fibres and fumes, employers must provide you with the correct type of respiratory (breathing) protective equipment (RPE).

The choice of RPE will depend upon the nature of hazard from which protection is required. In many cases RPE will only protect against one type of hazard (for example dust), although combined protection RPE is also available. Colour coding is often used to show what the equipment will protect against.

You should be shown how to put on, adjust and maintain any RPE.

 If you are issued with RPE, your employer should arrange for it to be face-fit tested, to ensure it fits and functions correctly.

☑ Where dust cannot be avoided you must wear suitable RPE (masks).

☑ If wearing any mask it should have a BS EN number and/or CE mark printed on it.

☑ Disposable masks should have at least two adjustable straps and may have a flexible nose band to shape around the bridge of your nose.

☑ There should be a good seal between the facepiece and your skin. Facial hair and other PPE can interfere with the fit.

 Cheap disposable dust masks from DIY stores offer little or no protection.

Other types are half or full face respirators with replacement filter cartridges.

☑ RPE should have a filter rating **FFP3, FFP2 or FFP1**. The filters can protect against different hazards (such as dusts or vapours).

- **FFP3** will offer the maximum protection. These reduce the dust you breathe in by a factor of 20.
- **FFP2** are good for medium risk. These reduce the amount of dust you breathe in by a factor of 10.
- **FFP1** are suitable for light duty work (such as sweeping up). These reduce the amount of dust you breathe in by a factor of four.

 For a protection factor of 20 (FFP3), for every 20 dust particles outside of the mask it is predicted that one would pass through the filter material.

FFP1 or FFP2 masks are unlikely to give enough protection against hazardous dusts, and should only be used for nuisance dusts. The seal should be tight against your face. Facial hair can reduce the effectiveness of the RPE. You should be clean shaven at the start of each shift to make sure the RPE seals properly against your skin.

Your risk assessment or COSHH assessment should say what type of filter you need.

 If in any doubt – ask. You have the right not to breathe in harmful dusts and fumes.

Protect today – breathe easily tomorrow.

Disposable half mask respirator

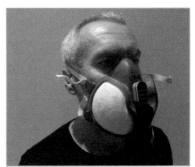

Combined hazard reusable filtering facepiece. (The colour coding on the nosepiece shows what it provides protection against)

06
Asbestos

What your site and employer should do for you

1. Make sure that information about the location of asbestos is made available to the workforce and others who may be affected.

2. Provide you with suitable training, relevant to the level of work being carried out.

3. Develop suitable control measures to manage your exposure and provide appropriate personal protective equipment (PPE), where required.

4. Arrange for health surveillance where legislation or policy requires it.

5. Provide supervision to make sure the control measures are being used properly.

B
06

What you should do for your site and employer

1. Follow any system of work that your employer has in place.

2. Make sure that you wear any PPE properly.

3. Stop work, keep away and warn others if you think you have discovered asbestos.

4. Never assume that all of the asbestos located in a building has been found.

5. Attend health surveillance, when requested by your employer.

Introduction

Asbestos is a harmful substance that continues to kill many people every year. It is the biggest occupational killer in the UK.

Microscopic asbestos fibres are invisible and are easily disturbed.

Breathing in any type of asbestos fibre can lead to lung diseases (such as mesothelioma, asbestosis and lung cancer).

 Around 5,000 people die each year as a result of past exposure to asbestos.

Where you will find asbestos

It has been estimated that asbestos was included in over 5,000 construction products in the 1940s to the 1980s. These materials mainly consisted of the following.

Asbestos flue

- ☑ Sprayed coatings to ceilings, columns and beams.

- ☑ Lagging of boilers, pipework or ducting.

- ☑ Pipework and boiler gaskets.

- ☑ Suspended ceiling tiles and floor tiles.

- ☑ Partitions and ceilings.

- ☑ Soffit panels and window boards.

- ☑ Asbestos cement roofing sheets, water tanks and pipes.

- ☑ Asbestos cement used as permanent formwork.

 Any building constructed before 2000 must, by law, be considered as potentially containing asbestos, and must be subject to an appropriate survey.

Asbestos is often hidden above suspended ceilings and behind walls. Workers should assume that asbestos may still be present, even after a survey has been completed.

If you think that you have discovered or disturbed asbestos, you must make sure of the following.

- ☑ Stop work immediately.

- ☑ Warn others nearby to keep away.

- ☑ Tell your supervisor or employer.

Asbestos surveys

An asbestos survey should be undertaken before work starts. There are two types of asbestos survey.

☑ **Management survey.** To assess how to manage and protect asbestos in an occupied building. ·

☑ **Refurbishment or demolition survey.** This must be undertaken before any invasive construction work starts. This survey is much more comprehensive than a management survey.

Asbestos can only be correctly identified by getting a sample analysed in a laboratory.

 In the absence of a laboratory report, it must be assumed that the material contains asbestos.

Working with asbestos

Any worker who is due to work in a building that is likely to contain asbestos must undertake a suitable asbestos awareness course before starting work.

Workers may come into contact with asbestos when undertaking maintenance, refurbishment or demolition work, such as the following.

☑ Modifying the structure (partial demolition).

☑ Stripping out.

☑ Installing new plumbing, electrics, windows and soffits, loft insulation, kitchens and bathrooms.

Never attempt to work on asbestos unless you are competent and equipped to do so, and licenced, if necessary.

All work with asbestos requires a written assessment of risk, appropriate levels of precaution (such as the use of personal protective equipment) and appropriate training.

Asbestos warning label

B 06

Asbestos removal

Projects can be categorised in the following ways.

☑ Licensed asbestos work.

☑ Notifiable non-licensed work.

☑ Non-licensed work.

The removal of high risk asbestos containing materials (such as sprayed asbestos, asbestos lagging and asbestos insulating board) must be carried out by a licensed contractor.

The removal of low risk asbestos containing materials (such as asbestos cement products and vinyl floor tiles) would not normally require a licence, providing that the correct precautions are taken (such as wearing the correct respiratory protective equipment). Training must be provided to all employees undertaking this work.

B
06

Damaged asbestos lagging

Labelled encapsulated asbestos

 You must be given awareness training if you are liable to disturb asbestos whilst carrying out your normal everyday work.

B
06

07

Dust and fumes (Respiratory hazards)

What your site and employer should do for you

1. Make sure that respiratory hazards (such as dust, fumes and vapours) are either eliminated or minimised.

2. Provide systems and equipment to make sure that exposures to respiratory hazards are reduced to the lowest level possible.

3. Provide information and training on the hazards and controls (such as on-tool extraction and wet cutting methods).

4. Issue you with the proper respiratory protective equipment (RPE) needed to protect your health, and train you how to use it properly.

B
07

What you should do for your site and employer

1. Make sure you know how respiratory hazards can damage your long-term health.

2. Follow the safe system of work given for the tasks you are carrying out.

3. Use any equipment provided to make the task safer (such as on-tool extraction methods).

4. Wear your RPE properly, and replace it as necessary.

5. Ask, if in any doubt, and report any changes in your health or problems with protective equipment.

Introduction

Respiratory hazards are substances in the air (such as construction dust) that can be inhaled and can lead to a range of illnesses and diseases. The damage is mainly to the lungs and airways, and includes lung cancer and silicosis. However, some respiratory hazards can also result in diseases in other parts of the body, such as the kidneys and liver.

 The Health and Safety Executive estimates that around 600 construction workers die each year from silica-related lung diseases. Much of this exposure comes from activities such as cutting paving slabs, blocks or kerbs.

As well as deaths from respiratory hazards, many more workers suffer chronic debilitating health conditions (such as occupational asthma) from breathing in hazardous substances on site. Many are forced to leave the industry due to work-related ill health.

B
07

The effects of exposure to most respiratory hazards are not always immediate. You may go home from work feeling more or less the same each day and don't realise that you have been exposed to a substance that may cause problems in the future.

As you are repeatedly exposed to small doses of dust, fumes and vapours they start to damage your body. The effects of these small doses build up over time. It can take months or years before symptoms of exposure become a problem to you and by then irreversible damage may well have occurred.

 At any one time there are far more people off work through occupational ill health than there are because of a work-related accident.

Exposure to everyday hazards, including wood dusts, flux, welding fumes, dusts from slab cutting, asbestos and many more common workplace materials and processes, can cause ill health.

Some dusts and fumes, known as respiratory sensitisers, can cause workers to develop asthma if inhaled regularly over a period of time.

As an industry we are exposed to many materials and products and are therefore exposed to particular respiratory hazards (such as asbestos, cement, stone, silica, lead, fillers, MDF, plastics, epoxies and solvents).

Breathing in hazardous airborne substances can cause wheezing, coughing, breathlessness, bronchitis and other respiratory diseases, including various types of cancer.

Exposure to solvent vapours can cause acute (immediate) effects as well as chronic (long-term) illness. This means the exposed person can suffer headaches, dizziness, unconsciousness and even death if they are exposed to high concentrations of the vapour, particularly if exposed in a confined space.

Respiratory hazards

The following categories describe the main respiratory hazards that may be encountered on site.

Dust

Dust is produced when solid materials are broken down into finer particles. Generally, the finer the particles are, the more hazardous they are, since they can get deeper into the lungs. The most hazardous dust particles are invisible to the naked eye and stay suspended in the air for long periods.

Operative working with dust suppression to reduce airborne dust

☑ **Nuisance dust** has no particular harmful properties but, if inhaled in large enough quantities, can still be harmful and cause breathlessness, wheezing, coughing and irritation.

☑ **Asbestos** fibres in air are responsible for several forms of cancer, including lung cancer and mesothelioma, as well as asbestosis. The microscopic fibres are easily released into the air by disturbing asbestos containing materials (ACMs). Asbestos cannot be easily recognised in materials and is often missed on construction sites. *(For further information refer to Chapter B06 Asbestos.)*

☑ **Silica.** Respirable crystalline silica (RCS) are microscopic particles of silica found in many construction materials (such as paving slabs, blocks and kerbs). Prolonged exposure to silica dust can cause silicosis, lung cancer and other life-changing or life-shortening conditions. Fine silica dust is created when materials are sanded, cut or drilled.

☑ **Lead** is a toxic metal that can cause many ill health effects (such as mental disturbance, effects on the digestive system, and even coma). Breathing in lead dust is only one of the ways that lead can enter the body. It can also enter by ingestion and by inhaling fumes from vapourised lead. In construction, lead can be found in old paint, flashing and roofing materials.

☑ **Wood dust**, created by cutting and sanding, is particularly hazardous, causing a range of health effects, from sensitisation to cancer. Softwood dust is known to cause sensitisation (a form of allergic reaction). Hardwood is a known carcinogen, responsible for lung cancer and cancer of the nasal passages. Medium density fibreboard (MDF) is made from separated softwood fibres, hardwood fibres and glues. It can form a particularly fine dust when cut, which increases the likelihood of dangerous amounts being breathed in.

☑ **Dry pigeon dropping** accumulations are common on construction sites, particularly on demolition or redevelopment projects. Droppings often contain a number of bacterial and fungal biological hazards. If disturbed, they can release a hazardous airborne dust that can result in severe respiratory illness (such as psittacosis) that causes pneumonia. If work is to be carried out in an area where pigeons have been nesting or congregating, the area must be thoroughly decontaminated first, and those carrying out the decontamination must wear suitable respiratory protective equipment (RPE).

 Dust is by far the most common hazard on a construction site.

Fumes

Fumes are produced by the heating of metals to high temperatures (such as during welding and gas cutting). Fumes contain tiny metal particles that can be inhaled. Metal fume fever is one of the main illnesses caused by breathing in metal fumes. It is caused by inhaling fumes from the welding or hot working of a number of metals, particularly galvanised steel. It is an acute illness, causing flu-like symptoms.

Vehicle emissions

Vehicle emissions contain many hazardous substances, including toxic gases and particulates. Carbon monoxide may cause death quickly, particularly where engines are used in confined spaces where high concentrations of gas can build up. Sooty particles from diesel engines are very fine, and can penetrate deep into the lung, causing lung cancer. Avoiding the use of engine powered equipment (such as disc cutters and generators) in enclosed spaces will reduce the risk. However, where this cannot be avoided, adequate ventilation must be provided and carbon monoxide alarms should be used.

B
07

Personal carbon monoxide alarm

Gases

Gases are chemicals in their gaseous state at room temperature. They mix with the air we breathe, and are often toxic when inhaled. Hydrogen sulphide, for example, is given off by rotting organic substances (such as sewage and rotting vegetation). It can build up in confined spaces (such as sewers, drains, silos and slurry tanks). At sufficient concentrations it can cause unconsciousness within a few breaths, and death shortly afterwards. Other toxic gases often encountered in construction are carbon dioxide and carbon monoxide, although they usually only reach toxic concentrations when released into confined spaces.

Vapours

Vapours are the gaseous state of substances that are liquids or solids at room temperature. They usually form when a substance evaporates (for example, the vapour from glue or paint). Solvents are also used for many different construction processes and can release high levels of vapour. Vapours can build up quickly in confined spaces and can cause headaches, dizziness, collapse and, in rare cases, death. Long-term exposure to some solvent vapours can also cause chronic health effects (such as liver and lung damage).

Gases and vapours can build up quickly in confined spaces

Mists and aerosols

Mists and aerosols are fine droplets of liquid suspended in air. The droplets are often of respirable size, which means that, if inhaled, they can get deep into the lungs. Some examples of hazardous mists and aerosols are listed below.

☑ **Twin pack paints,** used for creating high-quality finishes, usually contain isocyanates, which are powerful respiratory sensitisers, as well as being respiratory irritants. They can cause acute symptoms (such as respiratory irritation and bronchitis), but they can also cause asthma if inhaled over a period of time.

☑ **Legionella** is a common bacteria in the environment. When aerosolised this can easily be inhaled, resulting in legionellosis, which is a potentially fatal form of pneumonia. In construction, water aerosols may arise from dust suppression systems and vehicle washes.

B
07

Controlling exposure to hazards

The following simple steps should be taken to protect you from respiratory hazards.

☑ **Avoid creating dust.** Choosing the right equipment or method of work can protect workers' lungs and potentially eliminate the risk altogether. Pre-order sized materials rather than cutting them on site or use a block splitter rather than a disc cutter as this creates less dust and is quicker.

☑ **Stop the dust getting into the air.** If creating dust cannot be eliminated then minimising the dust being released should be the priority. This can be done in two ways.

Using a water-fed cut-off saw whilst wearing respiratory protection

– **Dampening down or wet cutting.** This is the cheapest and most effective way of minimising exposure. Water helps to form a slurry that prevents the majority of dust becoming airborne. Not only does it reduce what is breathed in, but it also has the benefit of less cleaning up afterwards. It is important to keep the flow constant while wet cutting or grinding and to dampen down before clearing up.

– **Capturing the dust.** Some materials (such as wood) do not suit the use of water to suppress dusts, so dust extraction should be considered. When your employer purchases or hires tools they should make sure that they have on-tool extraction wherever possible. Cleaning dust from work areas and tools is far better if a vacuum is used rather than sweeping with a brush.

☑ **Wear respiratory protection.** Even the best control measures won't prevent dust generation completely, so RPE must always be worn, even if you are wet cutting or using extraction.

 Refer to Chapter B05 Personal protective equipment for further information about RPE.

08

Noise and vibration

What your site and employer should do for you

1. Make assessments to see if you are exposed to excessive levels of noise or vibration.

2. Provide you with sufficient training so you are clear about the hazards from noise and vibration.

3. Develop suitable control measures to manage your exposure and, for noise, provide appropriate hearing protection.

4. Arrange for health surveillance where your exposure dictates this is necessary.

5. Provide supervision to make sure the control measures are being used properly.

B
08

What you should do for your site and employer

1. Wear your hearing protection when needed.

2. Make sure that you wear your hearing protection properly.

3. Look after your hearing protection and get it replaced if it is lost or damaged.

4. When using hand-held vibrating tools do not exceed the daily safe time limit, if one has been specified.

5. Attend health surveillance, when requested by your employer.

6. Make sure you understand the damage that excessive noise and vibration can do to you.

Introduction to noise

Damage caused to your hearing by exposure to loud noise can be permanent. As well as hearing loss, many workers also suffer from constant ringing or buzzing noises in one or both ears. This is known as tinnitus and there is no cure.

Noise-induced hearing loss can build up over time. You may not notice the effects each day, but over a period of time your hearing can get worse from the noise you are exposed to at work. When hearing damage becomes significant you may notice the following.

- [✓] You start to turn the television up a bit more than you used to.

- [✓] You struggle to hear conversations or parts of words, particularly when there is background noise (such as in social situations).

B
08

There are various sources of noise on a construction site. Many of these are made by hand-held tools and can give high noise exposures because they are close to the user's ears.

Other sources of noise could include the following.

- [✓] Tools that you are using.

- [✓] Tools that other people are using nearby.

- [✓] Site equipment (such as generators).

- [✓] Plant (such as excavators and concrete breakers).

Damage can be caused by continuous noise (such as drills and breakers) and peak noise, usually from impacts (such as from cartridge-operated tools or piling rigs).

As well as causing hearing damage, excessive noise on a construction site can mask other noises (for example, warnings or the sound of vehicles approaching). This creates an additional hazard (such as being struck by site vehicles).

Employer responsibilities

Employers have a legal duty to make sure your hearing is not damaged at work. They can do this in the following ways.

- [✓] By keeping you away from the noisiest activities, wherever possible.

- [✓] By planning to do the work using the quietest methods available (such as cutting holes with rotary diamond cutters rather than chain drilling with hammer drills).

- [✓] By selecting and using the quietest equipment available (such as generators with silencing kits fitted).

Where the noise levels are not reduced enough using the methods above, your employer should provide you with hearing protection to further reduce your exposure.

Employers must also tell you about the risks from noise and provide information on how you should protect your hearing.

Hearing protection

There are two main types of hearing protection, each with its own advantages and disadvantages.

 When site rules, site signage or induction briefings tell you that you should wear hearing protection, make sure you wear it.

Earplugs

☑ These can be foam plugs, which may also be mounted to a band or cord.

☑ Must be fitted correctly so that they work properly, otherwise they have very little effect.

☑ Must be fitted with clean hands, otherwise dirt can get into the ears and cause infection and other problems.

☑ You should be shown how to fit earplugs properly.

Foam earplugs worn incorrectly

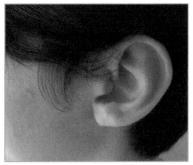
Foam earplugs worn correctly

Hearing defenders (earmuffs)

☑ These cover the whole of the ear and need to make a seal against the head to work properly.

☑ Can get hot and sweaty in hot weather, and can be uncomfortable to wear for long periods.

☑ Must be cleaned after use, or they can become unhygienic.

☑ Should be stored properly so they don't get dirty or damaged.

☑ Do not provide as much protection when worn over long hair or glasses.

 Whichever type of hearing protection you use, it must be worn all the time that you are exposed to high noise levels. Even short periods of not wearing protection has a huge effect on your daily exposure.

Noise action levels

The Noise at Work Regulations give two action levels that are daily exposures at which your employer must take action.

☑ **Lower exposure action level.** Your employer must make sure that appropriate hearing protection is available if your daily exposure is likely to be at or above 80 dB(A).

☑ **Upper exposure action level.** Your employer must make sure that you wear appropriate hearing protection if your daily exposure is likely to be at or above 85 dB(A).

 If you have to raise your voice to be heard by someone two metres away from you, then the noise level is about 80 dB(A). If the distance is one metre, then the noise level is likely to be about 85 dB(A).

B
08

A hand tool giving 95 dB(A) at your ear would result in you reaching the 80 db(A) action level in just 15 minutes, and the 85 dB(A) action level in under an hour.

A petrol cut-off saw giving 105 dB(A) at your ear would result in you reaching the 80 dB(A) action level in under two minutes, and the 85 dB(A) action level in around five minutes.

Introduction to vibration

Exposure to vibration can have serious health effects. Vibration from hand-held tools can cause hand-arm vibration syndrome (HAVS), which affects many workers in the construction industry. Whole-body vibration (WBV) also occurs in the construction industry and may, for example, affect drivers of construction vehicles, often resulting in back injury.

HAVS is a range of conditions caused by excessive exposure to vibration through the hands. These conditions are permanent and disabling. They affect the nerves, blood vessels, muscles, bones and other tissues of the hands and arms. Symptoms within the hands often include the following.

☑ Tingling. ☑ Loss of manual dexterity.

☑ Numbness. ☑ Painful throbbing.

☑ Loss of sensation.

There may also be muscle fatigue and loss of grip strength, as well as conditions such as carpal tunnel syndrome and tennis elbow.

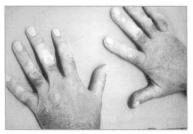

A common symptom of HAVS is finger blanching. This causes discolouration of the fingers, which may be temporary at first, but with longer exposure can become permanent.

People with HAVS often have problems with everyday tasks (such as fastening buttons). It is also painful, particularly when the hands are cold or damp.

Finger blanching caused by vibration

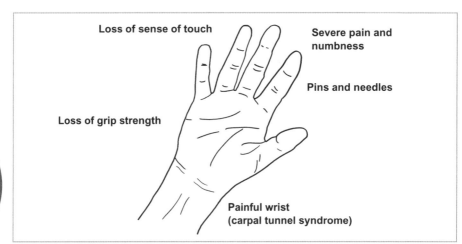

Loss of sense of touch

Severe pain and numbness

Pins and needles

Loss of grip strength

Painful wrist
(carpal tunnel syndrome)

Vibration related damage to the hands

 If you are diagnosed with HAVS you must inform your employer as they have a legal duty to report this to the Health and Safety Executive (HSE).

Equipment that can cause HAVS

HAVS is caused by prolonged use of hand-held equipment, where that equipment generates high levels of vibration. Typical equipment that produces enough vibration to cause HAVS includes the following.

☑ Compressed air breakers, rock drills, concrete pokers and scabblers.

☑ Hand-held drills, including hammer drills and rock drills.

☑ Disc cutters, angle grinders and wall chasers.

☑ Sanders, circular saws and planers.

☑ Plate compactors, strimmers and poker vibrators.

Your chance of getting HAVS depends on the vibration dose you receive each day. The dose is a combination of the amount of vibration produced by the tool and the time it is used each day. A common way of managing the risk from vibration in the construction industry is by limiting the daily dose of workers.

B
08

Managing vibration risks

Your employer has a duty to make sure that you are not exposed to levels of vibration that can damage your health. They must make sure of the following.

☑ Your risk of exposure to vibration is assessed.

☑ Put the following measures in place to control vibration.

  – Choose work methods that avoid exposing workers to vibration, such as the use of machine mounted rather than hand-held breakers.

  – Buy equipment that generates the lowest levels of vibration.

  – Make sure that equipment is well-maintained and attachments (such as bits and discs) are not excessively worn.

  – Limit the time you use vibrating equipment so that you do not receive a potentially damaging vibration dose.

☑ Give you information and training so that you know the risks from vibration.

☑ Provide you with health surveillance if you are exposed to significant levels of vibration.

B
08

Reducing vibration risks

Although your employer has a duty to protect your health, there are things (such as those below) that **you** can do to reduce the risk from vibration.

☑ Be aware of usage limits for vibrating tools, and make sure you do not exceed them.

☑ Keep your hands warm – cold hands are more prone to damage from vibration.

☑ Relax your grip and let the tool do the work. Applying too much force or gripping too tightly results in more vibration being transmitted to the hands.

☑ Take regular breaks when using vibrating tools, and during those breaks exercise your fingers to improve the blood supply.

Remember the following.

☑ Smokers are more likely to get HAVS than non-smokers (as smoking reduces circulation).

☑ Anti-vibration gloves, in some cases, are not very effective (although gloves may generally be useful in keeping the hands warm).

 The damage caused by exposure to excessive levels of vibration is permanent and could end your career.

B
08

09

Hazardous substances

What your site and employer should do for you

1. Use a less hazardous substance where possible.

2. Assess the risks of you using a substance.

3. Control exposure by providing a safe system of work.

4. Provide information and training on the risks and controls.

5. Monitor to make sure the controls are effective and provide health surveillance if needed.

B
09

What you should do for your site and employer

1. Follow the safe system of work/controls (COSHH assessment) and attend health surveillance sessions, where necessary.

2. Fully understand the hazards of using the substance.

3. Wear the correct PPE.

4. Tell the correct person of any incident or spill.

5. Store and dispose of the substance correctly.

Introduction

A hazardous substance can be described in the following ways.

☑ Any substance that could harm your health (such as solvents, cement and asbestos).

☑ Any dust, fibres or fumes given off by a work process.

☑ Any substance that could harm the environment.

How hazardous substances can affect your health

☑ **Immediate (acute)** – burns to the skin from acids or chemicals.

☑ **Long-term (chronic)** – developing cancer from asbestos exposure.

☑ **Disease** – contact with contaminated soil or water.

☑ **Sensitising** – over a period of time you start having more serious allergic reactions to less and less exposure to the substance.

B
09

How hazardous substances get into your body (routes of entry)

☑ **Inhalation** – breathing in dust, fumes, vapours and fibres.

☑ **Absorption** – contact with your skin or open sores/wounds in your body.

☑ **Ingestion** – being swallowed or eaten (usually from holding food with dirty hands).

☑ **Injection** – needles, sharps or high pressure (such as water jetting).

What your employer should be doing

Your employer should undertake the following under Control of Substances Hazardous to Health (COSHH) Regulations.

☑ Use a less hazardous substance if available.

☑ Read and understand the manufacturer's information on the substance.

☑ Carry out a risk assessment on how and where it is to be used.

☑ Put in place measures to control the exposure.

☑ Make sure you know the controls.

☑ Monitor to make sure the controls are effective.

 Some hazardous substances, such as fumes (welding), dust (cutting) or vapours (painting), do not have warning labels, as these are often created when you work. Your employer has a legal duty to assess these hazards too, and fill in a COSHH assessment as part of your safe system of work.

Your employer may ask you to attend regular health surveillance sessions, which you have a duty to attend.

 Health surveillance **is a system of ongoing health checks to detect possible ill health effects at an early stage.**

Employers can then introduce better controls to prevent any ill health effects from getting worse.

Identifying hazardous substances

The packaging or container of hazardous substances will carry one or more symbol, to indicate its hazardous properties. International pictographs were introduced in 2009. These are similar to the European symbols that they replaced, but they are a different colour and shape. Some of the new pictographs are shown in the table below.

Globally harmonised pictograms			
	Toxic (can be fatal) if swallowed or inhaled.		Hazardous to the environment and aquatic life.
	Contains gases under pressure. May explode if heated and can cause burns.		Oxidising gases, liquids and solids. May cause or intensify fire.
	Harmful skin, eye or respiratory irritation. May cause an allergic reaction, drowsiness or breathing difficulties.		Damage to organs and may cause serious longer-term health hazards (such as carcinogenicity and respiratory sensitisation).
	Flammable gases, liquids, solids and aerosols. Heating may cause a fire.		Corrosive and can cause severe skin damage or burns.
	Heating may cause an explosion.		

 If you find a substance in a container with no label, make sure that no-one else can come into contact with it and report it to your supervisor.

Disposal of hazardous substances

Hazardous substances can also contaminate land, drains, sewers, rivers and the air.

You should **never** mix them with general (non-hazardous) waste, pour them down drains, sinks or onto the ground, or bury, burn or fly tip them.

 Your site or employer should have a procedure to dispose of hazardous waste, including empty or part-used containers.

Highly flammable liquids

Highly flammable liquids (HFLs), such as thinners, solvents, petrol and adhesives, can easily catch fire and burn fiercely.

They can be identified by the following symbols.

If you have to use HFLs you must make sure of the following.

☑ Check there are no naked flames or other sources of ignition nearby.

☑ Only take the amount needed with you.

☑ Always follow the storage procedures.

☑ Have the correct fire extinguisher at hand.

 If a fire extinguisher could be needed during hot work activities then you should be trained to use it.

Liquid petroleum gas

Liquid petroleum gas (LPG) is a highly flammable gas. It is heavier than air so can sink into excavations, basements, drains, and so on.

It must be stored upright in a well-ventilated area and in a secure cage.

There are separate regulations covering the safe carrying of LPG bottles in vehicles.

B
09

LPG has a distinctive smell. If you think there might be a leak make sure of the following.

☑ Others are warned to evacuate the area.

☑ Carry out the following only if it is safe to do so.

    – Turn the cylinder supply valve off.

    – Open doors and windows.

    – Eliminate any source of ignition.

☑ It is reported immediately.

Gas from a leaking LPG bottle can expand to 250 times its bottle volume. It can catch fire at some distance from the original leak.

B
09

10
Manual handling

What your site and employer should do for you

1. Identify work activities that pose a manual handling risk.

2. Avoid the need for hazardous manual handling.

3. Identify the risks to your health from the manual handling of any load.

4. If the manual handling task has to be done then you must be provided with the equipment and a safe method of work to minimise any risk of injury.

5. Ask you how you would do the manual handling task (consultation).

6. Provide any necessary equipment and training.

7. Provide slip/trip free access routes and adequate lighting levels.

8. Help by planning delivery, off-loading and distribution of your materials and equipment to avoid unnecessary carrying and lifting.

What you should do for your site and employer

1. Follow the safe system of work.

2. Use lifting aids and equipment safely.

3. Co-operate with your employer. If in doubt, ask for advice.

4. Get help (two person lift), split the load and do not carry too much.

5. Make sure your activities do not put others at risk.

**B
10**

Introduction

 Manual handling **is the moving of any load by hand, including lifting, putting down, pushing, pulling or carrying by hand or bodily force.**

It is the construction industry's biggest cause of ill health.

Every year an estimated 900,000 working days are lost due to handling injuries.

Your back is strong but **repeated** twisting, straining and incorrect lifting techniques can, over time, lead to an injury.

Manual handling injuries resulting from unsafe or incorrect manual handling can affect the following parts of your body.

B
10

☑ Whole body.

☑ Arms.

☑ Back.

☑ Hands.

☑ Shoulders.

☑ Feet and ankles.

Back injuries are most common but hernias, ruptures, sprains and strains are all conditions that can result from manual handling.

Poor posture (such as slouching on the settee, sleeping on a poor supporting mattress, and sitting in a driving position that twists or doesn't support your spine) can all add to the problem.

Your employer has a legal duty to avoid any manual handling activity that will harm you.

Manual handling assessment

Where the assessment shows potential risks to the health of employees from the manual handling of loads, the employer must develop a safe system of work that avoids the risks. This requires attention to four main things.

☑ **Task.** What has to be achieved and by when?

☑ **Individual.** Are they male or female, large or small in stature and frame, what is their age and do they have any health issues or injuries?

☑ **Load.** Is it too heavy to lift, can it be broken down into smaller loads, or can two people lift it?

☑ **Environment.** What hazards are there on the route? For example, are there slippery or uneven floors, slopes, steps or narrow passages?

You can remember these four aspects as **TILE**.

Task

☑ Can manual handling be avoided completely?

☑ Does the task involve repetitive lifting?

☑ Can the distance a load has to be moved be reduced? (Get it delivered or moved nearer).

☑ Can lifting aids be used (for example a wheelbarrow, trolley or vacuum lifters)?

☑ How and from what height is the load to be lifted or lowered?

☑ Will it be necessary to over reach or stretch to put the load down?

☑ Does the task involve repetitive twisting while lifting a load?

B
10

Individual

☑ Do they need any manual handling training or the technique for the equipment?

☑ Are they male or female, tall or small, young or old?

☑ Are there any earlier injuries or health conditions?

Load

☑ Can the load be split down into smaller loads?

☑ Can it be moved by two (or more) people?

☑ Is the weight of the load known?

☑ Can it be gripped easily or are there adequate handholds?

☑ Where is its centre of gravity – is the load top heavy or an uneven weight?

Environment

☑ Is the floor or ground free from slip or trip hazards?

☑ Does the load need to be carried up steps or stairs?

☑ Are there any space constraints?

☑ Is the level of lighting adequate?

Team lifting

If the load is large, heavy or awkward get assistance, preferably from someone of about the same size and build as yourself to help maintain the balance of the load during lifting. Team lifting should only be carried out with people of similar capabilities.

 The only way to avoid manual handling is to use mechanical handling equipment (such as cranes, forklifts, goods hoists and jacks).

Lifting and handling

Good practice method of lifting (kinetic method)

(1) Bend at the knees   (2) Grasp the load   (3) Lift, using the legs   (4) Carry the load

B
10

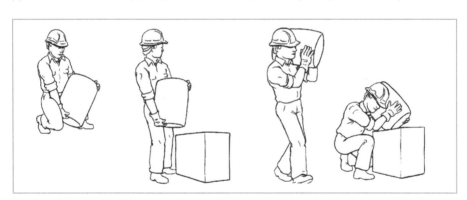

Good practice method for lifting and placing a load

Use your body wisely (kinetic method)

☑ Let your leg and thigh muscles do the work.

☑ Try to maintain the natural curve of your spine and relax your muscles.

☑ Use the movement of your own body weight to get things moving.

☑ Avoid flexing your back any further once you have started to lift.

☑ Do not snatch the load as you lift.

☑ Avoid leaning sideways or twisting your back, especially when your back is bent.

B
10

11

Safety signs

What your site and employer should do for you

1. Make sure safety signs follow standard designs (not handwritten signs).

2. Maintain signs and make them clearly visible.

3. Provide signs that are suitable for the hazard or risk.

4. Remove signs if they are no longer needed.

5. Display any safety sign identified in your safe system of work.

What you should do for your site and employer

1. Understand what signs and signals mean.

2. Speak to your supervisor if you are confused by a sign, there seems to be too many signs or your work area needs extra signage.

3. Follow the instruction or direction on any sign or signal.

4. Do not vandalise or remove any sign.

5. Report any damaged or missing signs.

**C
11**

Mandatory signs – must do

General mandatory

Safety harness must
be worn

Safety helmet must
be worn

Eye protection must
be worn

Safety boots must be worn

Safety gloves must
be worn

**C
11**

Prohibition signs – must not do

No pedestrians

No smoking

No escape route

No mobile phones

**Children must
not play on
this site**

**Scaffolding
incomplete
Do not use**

Warning signs

General warning

Forklifts at work

Flammable

Explosive

Corrosive

Toxic

Danger of electrocution

Fragile roof

Radioactive

Laser beams

Emergency escape and first aid signs – safe conditions

Emergency escape route signs

First aid signs

C
11

Assembly point

First aid

Wash your hands

Emergency eyewash

Emergency shower

Fire-fighting signs

Fire hose

Ladder

Fire point

Emergency fire telephone

Fire extinguisher

Call point

C
11

12

Fire prevention and control

What your site and employer should do for you

1. Put in place a fire prevention and fire action plan.

2. Explain the fire risks and controls.

3. Provide and maintain fire detection, fire-fighting equipment, clear escape routes and fire exits.

4. Have a system to control 'hot work'.

5. Provide means to make sure rubbish and waste doesn't build up.

What you should do for your site and employer

1. Practise good housekeeping and clear up your waste.

2. Get a hot-work permit whenever you might create sparks, heat or flames.

3. Keep exit routes and fire points clear at all times.

4. Store materials and fuels in designated areas.

5. Know what to do and how to raise the alarm if there is a fire.

C
12

Introduction

Fire kills about 350 people every year in the UK and injures many more. Depending upon the stage of construction or refurbishment, sites can be at a higher risk and fire and smoke can spread rapidly.

Fire

How fire starts

For fire to start there must be three elements (the fire triangle).

☑ Heat or ignition (such as a spark).

☑ Fuel (something flammable).

☑ Oxygen (air).

Fighting fire

Fire-fighting equipment works by removing the following aspects.

☑ Heat (cooling with water).

☑ The fuel.

☑ Oxygen (smothering with foam or a fire blanket).

The fire triangle

C
12

Hot works

Hot work can be any work where heat, sparks or naked flames are produced (such as welding, grinding or soldering).

Fire marshals should be informed of any hot works taking place as there would be a greater likelihood of a fire, they will need to ensure that affected areas are clear of people in the event of a fire.

What a hot-work permit will tell you

☑ When to start.

☑ How to prevent hot sparks spreading.

☑ Which type of fire extinguisher you should have available.

☑ If you need a fire watch.

☑ When you must stop.

☑ When you must go back and recheck (one or two hours after hot work ends).

 You should be informed of fire safety and evacuation procedures during your site induction (for example, means of raising the alarm and location of assembly points).

Portable fire extinguishers

When using portable fire extinguishers it is vital that everyone is vigilant and any hot work is controlled. The table below shows the types of portable fire extinguishers and what to use them on.

Extinguishing medium	Colour of panel	Where not to use
Water: for wood, paper, textile and solid material fires	Red	Do not use on liquid, electrical or metal fires
Foam: for liquid fires	Cream	Do not use on electrical or metal fires
Powder: for liquid and electrical fires	Blue	Do not use on metal fires
Carbon dioxide: for liquid and electrical fires	Black	Do not use on metal fires
Wet chemical: for wood, paper, textile, cooking oil and solid material fires	Yellow	Do not use on liquid, gas or electrical fires

Note: dry powder extinguishers may be provided as well as or substituted for water, foam or carbon dioxide extinguishers. Extinguishers used to control Class B fires (flammable liquids) will not work on Class F fires (cooking oils) because of the high temperatures produced.

C
12

13

Electrical safety, tools and equipment

What your site and employer should do for you

1. Provide safe, temporary electrics and safety lighting.

2. Isolate and protect from main, underground and overhead supplies.

3. Provide the right tools, equipment and PPE for the job.

4. Provide information and training so you know how to use them safely.

5. Make sure electrical installations, tools and equipment are inspected and maintained.

What you should do for your site and employer

1. Only use electrical tools or equipment, as selected for you by your employer, in accordance with your safe system of work.

2. Use the correct equipment and PPE, and carry out pre-use checks.

3. Only use tools and equipment if you have had the correct training.

4. Report any damage or faults.

C
13

Introduction to electricity

You can't see it. You can't smell it. It is dangerous and it can kill.

☑ There is no visible way of knowing for sure if a cable or wires are live.

☑ If there are cables or wires near where you are working, assume they are live and report them.

☑ The temporary nature of site electrical distribution systems and the possibility of them being damaged are all the more reason to be careful with electricity.

Electrical voltages

Battery power

☑ Battery-powered tools are by far the safest option.

☑ The severity of any electric shock will be much lower.

☑ There are no trailing leads.

☑ A lot of sites now provide secure battery charging lockers.

C
13

110 volt – yellow

☑ The standard colour code for 110 volt equipment is yellow.

☑ Electrical tools should be a maximum of 110 volt on construction sites.

☑ The 110 volt system means you would only get a 55 volt shock.

☑ You would feel an electric shock from faulty 110 volt equipment but no lasting damage should be done.

230 volt – blue

☑ The standard colour for 230 volt outdoor use is blue.

☑ It is commonly used for generators and electrical distribution.

☑ Domestic voltage or mains power is 230 volts.

☑ You will get a severe or even fatal electric shock if you touch a live 230 volt cable.

☑ This is why 230 volt tools are banned on most sites.

400 volt – red

☑ The standard colour for 400 volt is red.

☑ It is for equipment needing a lot of power (such as a tower crane).

 Electricity can kill. If in doubt, stop work and report any concerns to your supervisor.

Using extension leads and cables

☑ Always fully unwind an extension reel or cable.

☑ A part unwound cable can overheat, melt and catch fire.

☑ Where possible, route cables or leads overhead.

☑ Cables on the floor are trip hazards.

☑ Use protective ramps to protect cables from being run over if they need to be routed at floor level.

☑ Don't route cables across puddles or waterlogged ground.

☑ Get a transformer moved rather than using several leads joined together.

Electrical hazards

☑ There may be overhead power lines on site, which are only completely safe if switched off.

☑ People have been electrocuted and killed when items (such as ladders, towers or mobile plant) accidently touch or come close to them.

☑ If a fuse blows, check equipment and leads for damage first.

☑ If you see smoke from a power tool, switch it off and take it out of use.

☑ Burn, scorch marks or burning odours indicate an electrical fault.

☑ Damaged leads and cables, even if it is just the outer sheathing, must be taken out of use.

Protection devices

☑ You must use a residual current device (RCD) with any 230 volt tool and only after getting permission.

☑ RCDs work by cutting the power quickly if there is a fault.

☑ Portable RCDs fit between the plug and the socket.

☑ Test portable RCDs by pressing the test button daily and before use.

☑ Portable RCDs should have a combined inspection and test before first use and then every month.

☑ They must be kept free of moisture and dirt and protected against vibration and mechanical damage.

Portable appliance testing

☑ HSE guidance recommends that tools, leads and equipment should be tested every three months if used on site.

☑ If used, the portable appliance testing (PAT) label will tell you when the next safety check is due.

Introduction to hand-held tools and equipment

Many types of power tools and hand tools are used in the construction industry. Thousands of injuries occur from the use of hand-held tools and equipment.

Moving parts, rotating blades and drill bits can cause serious injury in an instant, as can non-powered hand tools (such as handsaws, trimming knives and hammers).

Because they are used regularly you can become complacent to the hazards and risks.

Noise and vibration from using hand-held tools and equipment can pose a risk to health.

 Refer to Chapter B08 Noise and vibration for further information.

Safe methods of working

Competence

To operate powered hand tools and equipment you must be competent.

☑ You must be trained to use certain tools.

☑ You need knowledge of the tool and the hazards associated with its use.

☑ You need experience gained by using the tool.

☑ You must have an understanding of the environment the tool is to be used in and its limitations.

Before using any tool or equipment

☑ Check it's the right tool for the job.

☑ Make sure it has been maintained.

☑ Carry out a pre-use visual check.

 The correct tools, equipment and PPE needed should be listed in your safe system of work.

Guards and safety features

☑ Always isolate the power and remove the plug from the socket when changing bits, blades or adjusting guards on power tools.

☑ Make sure all guards or other safety features (such as emergency stops) are in place and work.

☑ Adjust the guard so you can see what you are doing and to minimise the gap between it and the moving part.

☑ Never carry out any makeshift repairs or modifications.

C
13

Protect yourself

☑ Most power tool noise levels mean you should be wearing hearing protection.

☑ Do not exceed daily safe vibration exposure times.

☑ Wear the correct eye protection.

☑ Avoid loose clothing and neck drawstrings and make sure the power lead doesn't get entangled in moving parts, which can cause serious injury.

☑ Keep hands away from moving parts. Gloved fingers which have a good grip can 'stick' to a drill chuck, wrenching your fingers around it instantly.

Types of hand-held equipment

Petrol-driven hand tools

☑ Petrol must be kept in small quantities in approved containers.

☑ Refuel only in well-ventilated areas using a funnel.

☑ Do not refuel with the engine running or while parts are still hot.

☑ Exhaust fumes are toxic and must not be allowed to accumulate in enclosed or confined spaces.

Abrasive wheels and diamond blades

☑ The following are common types of machine.

    – Petrol cut off saws (disc cutters).   – Masonry bench saws.

    – Angle grinders.   – Wall chasers and floor saws.

    – Tile cutters.

☑ Abrasive wheels and diamond blades can burst, shatter or suffer high speed segment loss if not used correctly, resulting in serious injury.

☑ You must be trained, competent and authorised to change or mount a wheel or blade.

☑ The speed of the wheel or blade must match the machine speed.

☑ Only cut material the wheel or blade is made for.

☑ Diamond blades can fail in lots of different ways if misused.

☑ Diamond blade manufacturers supply free inspection and fault-finding guides.

☑ High-impact eye protection must be worn.

Wear the appropriate PPE and ensure the guards are properly set

C
13

Using a concrete diamond blade on tarmac can seriously weaken the blade. The result is that nail-sized segments can fly off at high speeds (approximately 180 mph).

Electrical hand tools

☑ All electrical hand tools used on site should only be 110 volts.

☑ Before every use you should carry out a brief visual inspection of the:
  - power lead and plug
  - casing
  - switches, triggers and guards.

☑ You must switch off and remove the plug before carrying out any adjustments.

Cartridge-operated tools

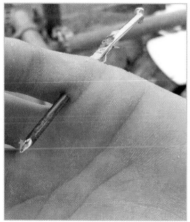

Poor practice and lack of concentration can lead to injuries

☑ These work like a gun by firing an explosive charge.

☑ They are used to fire fixings into solid surfaces (such as concrete or steel columns).

☑ These are dangerous in untrained hands.

☑ You must be trained and authorised to use a cartridge-operated tool.

☑ Tool manufacturers often offer free on-site training.

☑ Cartridge-operated tools need to be inspected, cleaned and lubricated regularly.

☑ High-impact eye protection and hearing protection must be worn.

C 13

Compressed gas tools (nail guns)

☑ They need to be inspected, cleaned and lubricated regularly.

☑ High-impact eye protection must be worn.

☑ Remove battery, fuel cell and remaining nails before clearing a blockage.

☑ Fuel cells or canisters must be disposed of correctly.

☑ Tool manufacturers often offer free, on-site training.

Chainsaws

☑ Chainsaws can inflict serious injuries.

☑ The main hazard is that they have a fully exposed cutting chain.

☑ Chainsaws can kick back (uncontrollably kick upwards towards the operator with the chain running).

☑ You must be fully trained, competent and authorised and wearing full chainsaw protective body clothing and head protection.

Compressed air-powered tools

☑ Compressed air tools are attached to a compressor using air hoses.

☑ Tools include heavy duty breakers, soil picks, concrete scabblers and pokers.

☑ Always check hose fittings are tight and secure before use.

☑ High pressure air hoses can cause serious injury if they break away from the compressor or tool. **Whip checks** should be used on every hose joint to prevent this.

Compressed air tools should be checked before and after use

Non-powered hand tools

☑ These may seem low risk, but are responsible for many injuries.

☑ They need to be well maintained and regularly inspected.

☑ Well used chisels and bolsters can form 'mushroom heads'. When they are struck fragments can fly into the air and into the eye.

☑ Loose handles, blunt blades and worn parts all pose a hazard.

Lasers

☑ If used correctly lasers should not pose a health hazard.

☑ A rotating laser means it's difficult to look directly at the beam for more than an instant.

☑ Static lasers (such as pipe lasers) pose more of a risk.

☑ Exclusion zones and warning signs must be in place if high-powered lasers are being used.

 Always follow the manufacturer's instructions when using any tool or equipment.

14

Site transport safety

What your site and employer should do for you

1. Explain the site traffic rules to you at induction.

2. Provide signage, markings, barriers and lighting.

3. Provide separate routes for pedestrians and vehicles.

4. Provide safe methods for deliveries, unloading and parking.

5. Arrange one-way systems and speed limits, and ban or control reversing.

What you should do for your site and employer

1. Follow all signs and speed limits.

2. Only use designated walking routes.

3. Discuss with the site manager first if you have to drive your vehicle on site.

4. Report any plant movement you think is unsafe or too close to your work.

5. Always wear your high-visibility clothing.

C
14

Introduction

The movement and operation of vehicles and plant causes many accidents and serious injuries on sites each year. The accidents involve not only the operator but people working close by or just walking past.

Mobile plant and site vehicles

The term *mobile plant* will be used in this section to cover all mobile plant and site vehicles that can move either under their own power or by being towed. Some examples are listed below.

☑ Dumpers.

☑ Excavators.

☑ Telehandlers and forklifts.

☑ Mobile cranes and piling rigs.

☑ HGVs, lorries and delivery wagons.

☑ Vans and cars.

☑ Road rollers, including pedestrian-operated rollers.

The term *operator* will be used to describe anyone driving or operating mobile plant and *pedestrians* will be anyone on foot.

Accidents

The most common types of accident are listed below.

☑ Being struck by reversing or moving mobile plant.

☑ Loss of control, overturning when working, travelling across or manoeuvring on slopes.

☑ People falling when climbing in or out of the machine.

☑ Accidental operation of mobile plant that has been left with the engine running – often occurring as operators are getting in or out of the machine.

☑ Being crushed between a structure and mobile plant as it moves or slews around.

Many accidents involving mobile plant happen because plant is large and the operator has a restricted view. Extra mirrors and CCTV are sometimes fitted to improve the operator's all-round vision – but don't depend upon it.

If you are close to moving or operating mobile plant you could be at risk. Whenever possible, stay within the designated pedestrian routes.

 A mobile crane slewing, an excavator digging or a lorry tipping material, whilst not travelling, can still be a danger if you get too close.

C
14

Never assume an operator will see you in time to avoid you.

At the very least, the movement of plant should be directed in situations where other people could be at risk, such as when a lorry is reversing or when a crane is carrying out a lift.

 A vehicle marshaller controls the movement of plant. A signaller controls the movement of a crane or load being lifted.

If you are the operator and you lose sight of the person directing you, you must stop and locate them before continuing.

 Do not try to operate any item of plant if you are not competent and authorised.

The chance of an accident between mobile plant and people on foot can increase after dark. Even when wearing high-visibility clothing, if the lighting is poor the operator may still not realise you are there. The use of working lights should improve safety.

 After dark and at other times when the light is not so good, remember that you will be harder to see.

C 14

Operator's field of vision is restricted

People have been seriously injured or killed when trying to pass too close to moving or reversing mobile plant.

Slewing plant

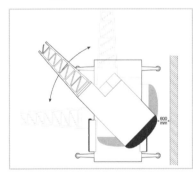

Clearance must take into account the reduced space if the crane tips

As the rear of a slewing crane or excavator turns, the gap between the rear of the machine and a fixed object (such as a wall, stack of materials or other plant) suddenly becomes much smaller (a **crush zone**).

☑ If the gap is 600 mm or less during slewing then the gap must be fenced or blocked off.

If you are operating plant (such as a pedestrian roller or MEWP), always be aware of what is behind or above – you may create your own crush zone.

This type of accident can happen because people on foot did not stay clear of mobile plant, took a short cut or followed a route that was not safe.

 Stay out of the crush zone. The shortest route may not be the safest route.

Management of mobile plant

A well-managed site will be organised to cut the chance of accidents between mobile plant and people on foot. Measures, such as the following, will be in place.

☑ Separate routes for mobile plant and people on foot with barriers between them.

☑ Separate site entrances for mobile plant and pedestrians.

☑ One-way systems and site speed limits.

☑ Turning areas, so that reversing is banned or minimised.

☑ Amber flashing beacons on mobile plant.

☑ A vehicle marshaller to control movement of mobile plant.

☑ All lights are working and switched on, where natural light levels are low and after dark.

☑ All vision aids (such as mirrors and CCTV) are clean and in good condition.

Whether you are an operator or not, the site rules on the safe operation and segregation of mobile plant should be explained to you during your site induction.

Working safely

C
14

☑ If you cannot avoid passing close to mobile plant, or if you need to speak to the operator, you will have to be patient and wait in a safe place until:

   – it has finished the job and stopped moving or working

   – it has moved away altogether

   – the operator knows that you are there, the plant stops operating and you are signalled to go past.

☑ Stay out of plant compounds and other parking areas unless you are authorised to be there. Be alert to plant starting up and moving off, and keep out of its way.

☑ Do not ask for or accept rides on plant that is not designed to carry passengers. Deaths have been caused by unauthorised passengers clinging onto an item of plant then losing their grip and falling under the wheels or tracks.

☑ Always wear your high-visibility clothing and keep it clean.

☑ Report any aspects of plant operations that you think are hazardous to your supervisor or employer. For example, where mobile plant:

   – is operating too close for comfort

   – travels or operates too fast and is a danger to other people

   – ignores one-way systems

   – uses routes that are only intended for pedestrians

   – looks to be defective.

Sometimes there isn't time to tell your supervisor or employer about a problem. If it's safe to do so, warn the operator and maybe others in the area. Your employer will still need to know about the problem. They can then make sure that the same situation does not happen again.

Dacorum LRC

**C
14**

15

Lifting operations

What your site and employer should do for you

1. Use only competent and authorised people to plan, supervise and carry out lifting operations.

2. Provide lift plans (safe systems of work) for all lifting operations and make sure that you are briefed and understand.

3. Provide information and training to all workers involved in lifting operations.

4. Make sure lifting equipment and accessories are suitable, inspected, maintained and examined.

5. Make sure equipment and accessories are marked with safe working loads.

What you should do for your site and employer

1. Follow any lift plan issued, or stop work and report it if you cannot.

2. Do not start work unless you fully understand your role.

3. Carry out pre-use checks on equipment and accessories that you have been issued.

4. Report any defects found on equipment or accessories before starting work.

5. Attend all briefings, as requested by your employer.

C
15

Introduction

Poorly planned lifting operations are often responsible for accidents. This can result in fatalities and injuries to those involved and/or the structural failure or overturning of the lifting equipment.

Your employer's duty regarding lifting operations include the items listed below.

☑ The lifting operation must be properly planned by a competent person (often referred to as the appointed person, whose role is to develop/approve the lifting plan).

☑ The lifting operation must be adequately supervised.

☑ The lifting operation must be carried out in a safe manner.

Lifting a generator using a lorry loader

Accidents involving cranes and other lifting equipment are often caused by one or more of the following.

☑ Using lifting equipment of the wrong type or lifting capacity.

☑ Using lifting equipment in an incorrect manner (unsafe technique).

☑ Incorrect slinging of the load.

☑ Lifting a load of an unknown and underestimated weight.

☑ Poor inspection and maintenance of the equipment or accessories.

☑ Failing to follow the lift plan (system of work) whilst carrying out the task.

☑ Poor assessment of ground conditions.

☑ Lack of training of the crane operators and signallers.

☑ Lack of co-ordination of crane movements when more than one crane is operating, and their arcs of movement overlap.

C
15

 Lifting equipment is any work equipment (such as cranes (mobile and static), hoists, telehandlers and excavators) that is used for mechanically lifting or lowering any load, including people.

Examples of lifting equipment

☑ Scaffold hoists.

☑ Passenger/goods hoists.

☑ Telehandlers.

☑ Excavators being used as a crane.

☑ Rough terrain forklifts.

☑ Crawler, mobile and tower cranes.

☑ Mobile elevating work platforms (MEWPs).

☑ Lorry loaders.

There should be a lift plan for operations being carried out by any form of lifting equipment. The depth of the plan will be reflected by the complexity of the operation. Work involving people at height or loads which are difficult to sling would be more complicated to plan.

A typical scaffold hoist

 Lifting accessories are items of equipment used for attaching the load to the lifting equipment (such as chains, ropes, slings, hooks, shackles, spreader-beams and eye bolts).

Planning a lifting operation

All lifting operations must be properly planned by a competent person who will decide how to safely conduct a lifting operation. This information will be recorded in a lift plan (safe system of work).

The lift plan will need to consider the following (this list is not exhaustive).

☑ Weight of load to be lifted.

☑ Type of lifting equipment to be used.

☑ Selection of lifting accessories (for example, chains and shackles).

☑ Overhead hazards (for example, power lines).

☑ Underground hazards (for example, cellars or underground voids).

☑ Level of supervision required.

☑ Lifting team (for example, crane operators and slinger/signallers).

☑ Means of communication (for example, hand signals or two-way radios).

 If you are involved in any lifting operation you must be briefed on the contents of the lift plan before work starts.

Inspections

A competent person (normally the operator) must inspect all lifting equipment and accessories at suitable intervals (usually before first use and then weekly). The frequency and extent of the inspections will depend on the potential for failure of the item. The inspection should include visual checks and functional tests.

Thorough examination

This process is generally carried out by a qualified engineer and is a very in-depth inspection that generates a report on completion. The report should be kept on file at the same location as the equipment or accessory.

Lifting equipment must be thoroughly examined as outlined below.

☑ When it is first used (unless bought brand new).

☑ If it is installed, after installation but before use.

☑ If it is assembled, after assembly but before use.

☑ At intervals not exceeding 12 months.

 Lifting equipment, used for lifting persons, and all lifting accessories must be thoroughly examined every six months.

C
15

A MEWP should be subject to a thorough examination at least every six months

Hand signals for signallers

The following images are industry recognised hand signals for people directing the movement of lifting equipment.

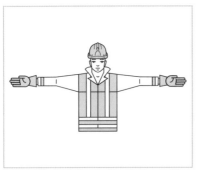

Start

Stop

Raise

Lower

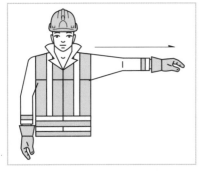

Left

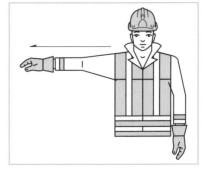

Right

 You must not signal plant operators unless you are trained and authorised to do so.

Horizontal distance (hands indicate the relevant distance)

Vertical distance

Move backwards

Move forwards

C 15

Danger

End (both hands are clasped at chest height)

 The signaller should stand in a secure position, where they can see the load and can be seen clearly by the lifting equipment operator. They should face the operator if possible. Each signal should be distinct and clear. These signals have been reproduced from Schedule 1 of Health and Safety (Signs and Signals) Regulations.

(This contains public sector information licensed under the Open Government Licence v2.0.)

C
15

16

Working at height

What your site and employer should do for you

1. Avoid the need to work at height if possible.

2. Provide a collective system to prevent falling (such as a scaffold, mobile elevating work platform (MEWP) or mobile tower).

3. Minimise any risk to you if there is a chance you could fall (such as by providing a harness or safety net).

4. Provide the correct work at height equipment and make sure it is inspected and maintained.

5. Give you information, instruction and training so you can work at height safely.

6. Make sure that all work at height is carried out in accordance with a safe system of work and that you are briefed fully.

What you should do for your site and employer

1. Follow the agreed safe system of work, and ask questions if you do not understand.

2. Use only equipment and methods you have been trained in.

3. Not misuse any equipment.

4. Not take risks or short cuts.

5. Stop and seek advice if anything changes or seems unsafe.

6. Make sure you carry out pre-use checks on your equipment.

D
16

Introduction

☑ On average 43 construction workers are killed each year due to accidents.

☑ The biggest killer (around half) is falls from height, with an average of seven people dying each year as a result of falling through fragile roofs.

☑ For over seven-day injuries, slips, trips and falls on the same level account for 21% and falls from height for 11%.

☑ Selecting the wrong type of work equipment results in many falls from height every year.

Many construction workers have sustained a life changing injury as a result of a fall from height. Such an event impacts not only the worker, but their family, lifestyle and ability to earn an income. It is vitally important that all work at height activities are adequately planned, assessed and the correct equipment selected and used to reduce the risk of injury.

 What can you fall from?

Many falls are from poorly secured ladders, faulty or poorly used stepladders or makeshift working platforms, which offer little or no fall protection.

About seven workers a year die after falling through fragile roofs. Others suffer serious injuries and disabilities as a result of falling.

For all work at height, measures must be taken to prevent the risk of any fall that could cause injury.

Work at height is work at **any** height where a person could fall and be injured. It also includes instances (such as working next to an open excavation) because of the risk of falling in.

D
16

What your employer should do

☑ Identify jobs that involve work at height.

☑ Plan the work to make sure that proper precautions and controls are in place.

☑ Choose and use the right equipment. This is often the equipment that protects the most people.

☑ Make sure that people working at height are competent, authorised, sufficiently experienced and that the work is adequately supervised.

☑ Communicate risk control measures to the workforce.

☑ Make sure the equipment is regularly inspected and maintained and that defective equipment is taken out of service.

Planning the work

☑ A risk assessment must be completed for all work at height.

☑ The following should be taken into account.

  − The complexity of the work being done.

  − Who is doing the work and for how long.

  − Weather conditions and surface conditions (such as a wet sloping roof).

  − How to raise and store materials and equipment.

☑ The emergency arrangements needed.

Hierarchy for working at height

Any person planning work at height should always follow a hierarchy of control and consider options at the top of the hierarchy before moving down.

> **Step 1. Avoid working at height**
> **e.g. assemble on the ground and lift into position using a crane or by fixing guard-rails to structural steelwork on the ground before lifting and fixing at height.**

> **Step 2. Prevent falls from occurring**
> **Use an existing safe place of work**
> **e.g. parapet walls, defined access points, a flat roof with existing edge protection**

> **Step 3. Prevent falls through providing *collective* protection**
> **e.g. scaffolding, edge protection, handrails, podium steps, mobile towers, MEWPs**

> **Step 4. Prevent falls through providing *personal* protection**
> **e.g. using a work restraint (travel restriction) system that prevents a worker getting into a fall position**

> **Step 5. Minimise the distance and/or consequences of a fall using *collective* protection**
> **e.g. safety netting, airbags or soft-landing systems**

> **Step 6. Minimise the distance and/or consequences of a fall using *personal* protection (The last resort)**
> **e.g. industrial rope access (working on a building façade) or a fall-arrest system using a high anchor point**

D
16

Requirements for working at height

☑ Safe access (such as a tower staircase or secured ladder) must be provided.

☑ Edge protection (such as temporary guard-rails) must be put in place.

☑ Surfaces can become slippery in wet or frosty conditions.

☑ If you are working on or near to a leading edge then measures (such as a physical barrier or safety net) should be installed. A harness and lanyard must only be used as a **last resort**.

☒ You should **not** work on any structure where there is no protection from falls.

Fragile roofs

There are many fatal and serious injuries from people falling through fragile roofs and roof lights.

The following items are likely to be fragile.

☑ Roof lights.

☑ Glass, including wired glass.

☑ Old liner panels on built-up sheeted roofs.

☑ Rotten chipboard.

☑ Fibre cement sheets.

☑ Slates and tiles.

☑ Metal sheets.

☑ Asbestos cement profiled roofing sheets.

Asbestos cement sheets are obvious, but fragile roof lights, which look like the more secure surrounding roof structure over time, are not so obvious.

Many people are not aware that parts of a roof are fragile.

 You should not assume that the roof will support your weight or try to walk near the underlying supports.

D
16

All fragile roofs should be considered to be unsafe unless additional protection has been provided. It is sometimes difficult to see a fragile surface, especially if a roof is dirty, weathered, covered by moss or has been painted. Buildings with a fragile roof covering should ideally show warning signage (as shown in the image below) but this will not always be the case.

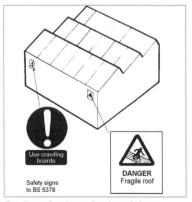

Fragile roof and crawling board signs

A safe system of work **must** be put in place, and as a priority, work on a roof should be avoided where possible (for example by working from underneath on a safe platform, using specially designed access equipment, or a MEWP). A safe system of work should also consider the following.

☑ Suitable access is provided (such as a stair tower or ladder) or accessing the area with a MEWP.

☑ Specialist working platforms with handrails are provided, which are designed to span the roof purlins and evenly distribute the loading applied.

☑ The installation of safety netting, crash decks or airbags underneath the roof.

☑ Safety harness anchor points.

☑ Physical barriers or covers around or on fragile surfaces (such as roof lights or sky lights).

☑ Arrangements for emergency situations, including how rescue will be carried out for casualties who have fallen into a safety net or are suspended by a harness.

 Never try to access or cross a fragile roof light without a safe system of work.

Voids and holes

All holes and voids (such as those listed below) where a person could fall any distance and injure themselves must be protected.

☑ Floor and roof openings.

☑ Floor joists and roof trusses.

☑ Lift shaft openings.

☑ Service holes and risers.

☑ Open manholes and other voids.

☑ Openings created during demolition.

☑ Open excavations.

☑ Openings created during site surveys.

All openings must be protected with secure barriers, covers, gates or doors, which are secured in position and display the right warning signs.

☑ Never remove a protective cover unless authorised to do so and you are protected against falling whilst the cover is being removed.

☑ If a hole, gap or void needs covering, you should report this to your supervisor straight away.

Properly constructed void protection, complete with appropriate signage

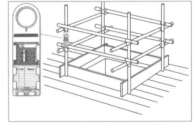

Scaffolding edge protection constructed around a void, complete with a scaffold tagging system

Preventing falls

If work at height cannot be avoided the best way to prevent people falling is by using physical barriers and equipment.

☑ Scaffolding, mobile access towers, MEWPs, podium steps and other proprietary edge protection systems.

☑ The minimum height of any guard-rail is 950 mm above the working platform.

☑ Any gap between the barrier and the working platform must not be greater than 470 mm.

☑ Plastic barriers, netting or rope and pins are not suitable as edge protection to prevent people from falling, unless they have been specifically designed for that purpose.

D
16

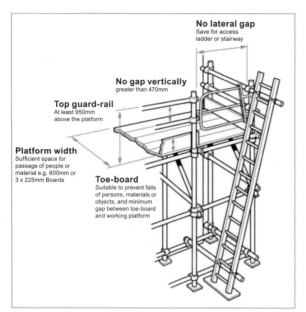

No lateral gap
Save for access
ladder or stairway

No gap vertically
greater than 470mm

Top guard-rail
At least 950mm
above the platform

Platform width
Sufficient space for
passage of people or
material e.g. 600mm or
3 x 225mm Boards

Toe-board
Suitable to prevent falls
of persons, materials or
objects, and minimum
gap between toe-board
and working platform

Physical barrier fall prevention

Arresting falls

Fall-arrest systems include safety harnesses, soft landing systems, safety netting and crash decks.

☑ If falls can't be prevented then the risk of injury must be minimised.

☑ Arresting falls must be considered a last resort and is only acceptable when other methods (further up the work at height hierarchy) have been considered and ruled out.

☑ The safe system of work must contain a procedure for emergency rescue.

Harnesses

Harnesses (personal) should only be used if falls can't be prevented by physical barriers or minimised by using collective arrest systems.

☑ Harnesses can be used to prevent a fall from occurring (fall restraint) and to minimise the consequences of a fall (fall arrest). Fall restraint is preferred to fall arrest.

☑ Choosing the type of harness and lanyard to be used is vital. Your employer should take into account where it is being used, how far the wearer may fall, any obstructions they may hit and any pendulum effect. (Swinging from side to side after the fall has been arrested.)

☑ You must receive training before using a harness and lanyard.

☑ It is vital you know how to inspect a harness for damage, how to fit it properly, where to attach it and where not to attach it.

A harness could be the one thing preventing you from falling to your death. Make sure you clip on at all times.

D
16

Never use a harness to work at height unless you have been trained.

There must be an effective rescue plan in place in case a person wearing a harness falls.

☑ They will need to be rescued quickly.

☑ When someone is arrested and suspended in a harness they can experience a condition known as suspension syncope (where the person suspended faints and could suffer further complications).

Types of access equipment

Mobile elevating work platforms

☑ Common types are scissor lifts and boom type (cherry pickers).

☑ You must only use a MEWP if you have been fully trained and are competent.

☑ If you are a passenger in a boom type MEWP you must wear a full body harness and restraint lanyard clipped to the designated attachment point in the basket.

☑ If the machine is fitted with additional ground level controls they should should only be used in an emergency (for example, power failure).

☒ **Never** clip onto a nearby structure.

☒ You must **never** stand on the guard-rails of the MEWP, lean out when ascending or descending, or climb out when in the elevated position.

Scaffolding

Good example of a warning incorporated into a physical barrier – do not access scaffolding if you see this sign

☑ Scaffolding must only be erected, altered or dismantled by trained and competent scaffolders.

☑ Any platform you are working on must have double guard-rails and toe-boards fitted.

☑ Keep the scaffold working platform clean and tidy.

☑ Brick guards must be fitted if materials are stored above toe-board height or if there is a risk of tools or materials falling and striking someone below.

☑ You should always follow the safe loading information.

☒ You must never interfere with scaffolds or remove any components, no matter how simple it appears to be.

☒ You must never overload scaffolds.

D
16

Mobile access tower scaffolds

Mobile access tower scaffolds are a safe and versatile form of access equipment if used correctly. Unfortunately, many towers are not erected or used correctly, can easily become unstable, and are the cause of many accidents every year.

You must hold a PASMA or equivalent qualification to erect, alter or dismantle a mobile access tower scaffold.

The training should cover how to reduce common risks associated with this type of equipment and include information on the following.

Safe working on a mobile tower, with toe-boards and guard-rails in position and wheels locked

☑ Manufacturer's instructions for safe use.

☑ Use of locking wheel brakes.

☑ Using only the internal ladder to access the deck.

☑ Checking that guard-rails and toe-boards are fitted (these must not be removed).

☑ Preventing over reaching.

☑ Assessing loading capability (how much weight can be placed on any platform).

You must make sure of the following.

☑ Working platforms are not fitted too high so that guard-rails are too low.

☑ Towers are not overloaded.

☑ The hatch is closed when working on the platform.

☑ It is positioned on level ground.

☑ It is not being used near overhead power lines.

D
16

 If you are only working on a mobile access tower scaffold and not involved in erecting, altering, dismantling or moving it, you should receive a toolbox talk on the risks and hazards associated with your work as a minimum. A toolbox talk will not give you the authority to erect, adapt, dismantle or move the tower.

Podium steps

Podium steps have become a popular piece of access equipment as they provide a safe and efficient means of achieving low level access.

They are a safe and versatile form of access equipment if used correctly.

They allow you to work from the working platform facing every side without becoming unstable.

They can be unstable and topple over if not built or used correctly.

Podium steps in use, correctly assembled and wheels locked

 You must always use the brakes when using the podium steps. Do not pull yourself along when you are inside it.

Stepladders

There are many types of stepladder on the market. Some offer good fall protection and others less so.

They should only be considered for light work of short duration (less than 30 minutes is recommended), and where the use of other, more suitable work equipment is not appropriate.

Wherever possible, platform steps should be the preferred option over traditional swing-back steps.

Stepladders should be used only when it is not possible to use other access methods.

Always check they are in good condition before use.

Always use on firm, level ground.

Always make sure they are fully extended and face forward towards the steps.

Three points of contact should be maintained where possible.

Report any defects to your supervisor.

Never over reach or apply a side loading.

Never stand on the top three treads of any stepladder unless it is designed to be used this way.

Stepladder with integrated side guard-rails for additional protection

D 16

Ladders

☑ Ladders should be considered as a **last resort.**

☑ They should only be considered for light work of short duration (less than 30 minutes is recommended) and where the use of other work equipment is not appropriate.

☑ They are most often misused when used as a working platform.

☑ It is essential that those who use ladders are trained and competent to do so.

☑ Always check they are in good condition before use.

☑ A painted ladder can hide defects or damaged parts.

☑ Report any defects to your supervisor.

☒ Ladders should not be used near power lines.

If ladders are used, they should meet the following criteria.

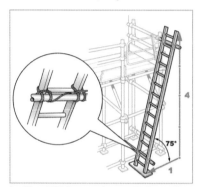

☑ Be of the correct type – Class 1 industrial.

☑ Be in good condition.

☑ Be placed on firm and level ground.

☑ Be properly secured (tied at the top).

☑ Use outriggers if available.

☑ Not be at risk of being struck by vehicles.

☑ Be set at the correct length and angle for the job – 75° or a ratio of **1:4 (one out to four up).**

☑ Extend one metre past the stepping off point.

Ladder at 75 degrees (one out to four up)

D
16

You should have three points of contact at all times.

Ladders are classified into the following three different grades.

☑ Class 1 industrial.

☑ BS EN 131 light trades.

☑ Class 3 domestic.

 Class 1 industrial ladders are recommended for use in construction environments as they offer the highest duty rating.

D
16

17

Excavations and confined spaces

What your site and employer should do for you

1. Make sure that you do not have to enter an excavation unless the sides have adequate support to prevent collapse.

2. Prevent people, materials and vehicles from falling into excavations.

3. If your job involves or creates a confined space, make sure this has been identified.

4. Assess the risks and develop a safe system of work.

5. Make sure that anyone entering a confined space is properly trained.

What you should do for your site and employer

1. Do not enter any excavation which is unsupported.

2. Install supports following the safe system of work.

3. Do not leave any open excavation unguarded.

4. Do not enter a confined space unless a safe system of work is in place and you are trained to do so.

5. Do not take any risks.

D
17

Introduction to excavations

An excavation is any hole or trench dug into the ground as part of construction or utility work. Some excavations are knee deep, but many are deeper. They do not need to be deep before becoming a serious risk or a confined space.

Every year deaths and injuries occur due to collapsing excavations, workers being overcome by poisonous gases or striking live services.

Excavations and trenches collapse for the following reasons.

☑ The sides are not supported or supports are not installed properly.

☑ Vehicles operate too close to the edge (for example dumpers, excavators and concrete wagons).

☑ Materials and spoil are stored too close to the edge.

☑ The ground dries out, shrinks and collapses.

☑ Heavy rain weakens the ground and the sides.

☑ The excavation undermines or weakens nearby walls and structures, which causes collapse.

 Excavations are dangerous

A cubic metre of soil can weigh over a tonne (1,000 kg).

A shallow excavation can easily collapse onto you if you are bending over.

It can easily crush your legs, hips or chest and prevent you breathing.

Collapse is silent and without warning.

D 17

Safe working in a deep excavation using trench boxes and a tied ladder

Examples of good practice are listed below.

☑ Avoid the need for anyone to go into an excavation.

☑ Install excavation supports before anyone goes into an excavation.

☑ Use methods that protect the person installing the support system.

☑ Only work within the safety of the protected area on long open excavations (for example within the confines of a drag box or trench supports).

☑ Provide a safe way to get in and out (such as a tied ladder).

☑ Provide fall prevention around the excavation (such as a handrail or extended trench sheets).

☑ Prevent vehicles from coming too close (for example using wheel stop blocks).

A competent person must inspect the excavation before the start of each shift. Something may have happened to affect its stability or something may have fallen from or into it.

 Keep vehicles a safe distance away from the edge of an excavation. A full 6 m³ concrete wagon weighs 26 tonnes.

Poisonous or flammable gases and fumes

Poisonous gases and fumes (such as those listed below) can be heavier than air and can 'pour' over the edges and start filling up an excavation or a confined space.

☑ Exhaust fumes from petrol or diesel-powered plant.

☑ Naturally occurring gases (such as methane) which seep out of the ground.

☑ Fumes from solvents such as welding plastic pipes, epoxy resins or sealants.

☑ Liquefied petroleum gas (LPG) or pipe-freezing sprays.

Safe systems of work may include the following.

☑ Using a gas detector to test the air before entry and then monitoring continuously.

☑ Pumping in fresh air.

☑ Using a solvent-free product that does not give off fumes.

☑ Wearing breathing apparatus as a **last resort**.

 Always be aware of gas hazards

You may not be able to see or smell gas in an excavation or a confined space.

If you are in an excavation or a confined space and feel light headed, dizzy or can smell gas: warn others – get out – stay out – report it immediately.

D 17

Underground services

Underground services include the following.

☑ Electricity cables.

☑ Gas mains.

☑ Water mains.

☑ Sewers and drains.

☑ Telecommunications or fibre optics.

☑ Oil or fuel pipes.

Thousands of service strikes happen every year. Many result in serious injury and some are fatal. It is vital that any excavation work, no matter how big, small, deep or shallow, is properly planned.

Before digging, every effort should be made to locate existing services. These methods will show roughly where the services are.

☑ Refer to service drawings.

☑ Phone up the utility company.

☑ Carry out a ground radar survey.

☑ Use cable avoidance tool detection (such as CAT and Genny equipment).

Hand digging trial holes to expose the services is the most accurate way of locating them.

Examples of the services you are most likely to find and their relevant colours are shown below (this list is not exhaustive).

Service	Colour
Electricity (all voltages)	Black or red
Water	Blue, black or grey
Gas	Yellow
Communications	Grey, white, green, purple or black

Safe systems of work may include the following.

☑ Not using forks near live underground services.

☑ Always treating services as live unless confirmed otherwise.

☑ Never assuming a service runs in a straight line.

☑ Marker tape or tiles laid above services will warn of their presence.

If you find an unexpected underground service, report it immediately.

D
17

Underground services

 If you strike a live service – get out quickly, do not go back, warn others and report it.

Introduction to confined spaces

Workers can become trapped or overcome by fumes, vapours, explosive or poisonous gases when working in confined spaces. In many cases this can lead to the person dying.

 Many workers who attempted to rescue workmates without a proper rescue plan were also overcome by the gas and fumes themselves and have collapsed and died, adding to the tragedy.

What is a confined space?

Confined spaces are not just tanks or chambers. They do not have to be totally enclosed.

They can be any area where there is a risk of the following.

☑ Reduced or increased levels of oxygen in the air.

☑ The presence of poisonous gases or fumes.

☑ The presence of flammable or explosive gases or vapours.

Depending upon the work hazards many areas could be classed as a confined space. Some examples are listed below.

☑ Excavations and trenches.

☑ Manholes, inspection chambers, sewers and soakaways.

☑ Service tunnels, plant rooms and boiler rooms.

☑ Basements, voids and staircases.

☑ Lofts and attics.

☑ Unventilated rooms and rooms with closed windows and doors.

☑ Oil storage tanks or water tanks above ground.

An unventilated room may not seem like a confined space. However, if you are using a substance in the room that gives off hazardous vapours then you could quickly become unconscious.

Hazards

Reduced oxygen levels

Oxygen, which we need to breathe, can be reduced in the following ways.

☑ By hot works or machinery that burns up the oxygen.

☑ Through people breathing.

☑ By rust inside enclosed tanks.

D
17

Build up of poisonous or flammable gases

Oxygen can be replaced by poisonous or flammable gases by the following.

☑ Stirring up sludge or slurry in excavations.

☑ Natural methane from the ground or rotting vegetation.

☑ Using substances that give off fumes or vapours.

☑ Sewage giving off hydrogen sulphide (smells like rotting eggs).

☑ Chalky ground, which gives off carbon dioxide.

☑ People breathing out carbon dioxide.

☑ Gases (such as LPG, methane or oxygen enrichment) which build up to form a highly flammable atmosphere.

An overturned tanker or a large spill may release petrol or dangerous chemicals into the drainage system. The vapours can travel hundreds of metres.

Working in a confined space

Your employer should identify if the work activity, hazards and area of work mean it is classed as a confined space. Anyone working in a confined space must be trained.

Work in a confined space needs a minimum of three safety documents to form a safe system of work.

☑ Method statement including a rescue plan.

☑ Risk assessment.

☑ Permit to work (this manages entry and control).

D
17

Using protective equipment within a confined space

The safe system of work will identify important issues, such as those listed below.

☑ Who can enter and for how long (time limits).

☑ How to get in and out safely.

☑ What tools and materials to use and how.

☑ What personal protective equipment to use.

☑ The type of air monitoring equipment and alarm system.

☑ The emergency arrangements.

☑ The rescue equipment and trained rescue team.

The air must be constantly monitored before and during entry using a meter with an alarm. If the alarm sounds, the area must be evacuated as quickly as possible. Usually there is one person (called the 'topman') at the entrance to the confined space whose job is to get the rescue plan underway if things go wrong.

Never try to rescue someone unless you are part of a trained rescue team. Use the time to get expert help and call the emergency services.

D
17

18

Environmental awareness and waste control

What your site and employer should do for you

1. Explain any specific environmental issues at site induction.

2. Develop procedures for avoiding pollution and tell everyone involved.

3. Provide means to distribute, store and use materials to avoid damage.

4. Provide means to dispose of waste correctly.

5. Provide emergency response methods (such as spill kits).

What you should do for your site and employer

1. Reuse materials where possible.

2. Dispose of waste correctly.

3. Avoid creating too much dust or noise.

4. Turn off plant, equipment and taps when not in use.

5. Know where the spill kit is, how to use it and report any incidents.

E
18

Introduction

The construction industry is the single biggest consumer of resources in the UK, using around 420 million tonnes of materials each year. The industry also generates a huge amount of waste (around 120 million tonnes each year); about 20 million tonnes of waste still goes to landfill, including 10 million tonnes of new, unused building products.

The poor management of materials and resources on a construction project can lead to excessive amounts of waste. This can be costly, is bad for the environment and it can also be unsafe.

The following are some ways that waste can be generated.

☑ Poor design.

☑ Incorrect or over-ordering.

☑ Poor workmanship.

☑ Incorrect storage and management of materials leading to damage.

Sustainability

You will increasingly hear the word sustainability being used in connection with construction work. The drive to carry out construction in a sustainable way affects everyone in and around the industry.

One element of sustainability is to carry out construction work in a responsible way and to minimise environmental damage, which could otherwise cause problems for future generations.

Collecting rainwater for reuse

Examples of good practice are listed below.

☑ Using locally produced materials and minimising transportation of raw materials and finished goods.

☑ Using timber and other wood products that can be fully traced to sustainably managed forests.

☑ Looking after the people who carry out construction work and using local labour and services to support the local economy.

☑ Saving energy wherever possible by turning off equipment when not in use.

☑ Not damaging the environment by causing pollution.

☑ Designing out waste.

☑ Using reclaimed materials or materials with a high recycled content.

E
18

- ☑ Reusing left over materials wherever possible to conserve raw materials and save the energy it would take to produce new.

- ☑ Segregating waste into different types so that it may be reused or recycled more easily.

 Water, energy, fuel, construction materials and time are often wasted on construction sites, practices which need to be stopped or at least reduced.

Environmental responsibilities

Responsibilities of the person in charge of the site

The person in change of the site has contractual and legal responsibilities to make sure of the following.

- ☑ Environmental planning conditions are implemented.

- ☑ Environmental damage is prevented during construction.

- ☑ Harmful substances, including fuels, are stored and handled correctly to prevent spillage or pollution.

- ☑ Employees are trained how to use spillage response equipment (for example, spill kits).

- ☑ That materials are properly segregated into different types of waste.

- ☑ Only registered waste carriers are used.

- ☑ Waste is properly disposed of through licensed contractors and facilities.

- ☑ Correct records and documentation are kept for all waste.

They should also work out ways of preventing, reusing or recycling as much waste material as is practical in line with the waste hierarchy and industry commitments to reduce waste to landfill.

Your part in preventing environmental damage

You should be given instructions and advice during and after site induction so you understand the following.

- ☑ The environmental site rules (such as how to dispose of your waste).

- ☑ What damage your work can have on the surrounding environment.

- ☑ What work controls are needed to avoid damage.

- ☑ What you need to do as an individual.

- ☑ What to do in an emergency (for example, how to use a spill kit properly).

E 18

Pollution

Causes of pollution

☑ Deliberately or accidentally allowing substances (such as cement, silt, grout, sewage, chemicals, oils/greases or vehicle fuels) to soak into the ground or contaminate rivers, streams and ditches.

☑ Allowing smoke, fumes or dust to contaminate the air.

☑ Causing too much noise, light or vibration, which can affect the quality of life of people who live or work nearby.

☑ Not segregating contaminated materials from other waste (for example putting rags used to clean up an oil spillage in with general waste materials).

☑ Allowing noise, dust or other polluting substances to disturb or destroy the habitats of protected or invasive plants and species of wildlife.

Why pollution occurs

☑ Substances enter rivers, streams, ditches, drains or the ground because they aren't stored correctly.

☑ Not having the equipment or a plan to control accidental spillages.

☑ Rain and muddy surface water running off site onto roads, into drains and watercourses.

☑ Not having properly protected storage areas, to contain the leaks or spills of harmful liquids (such as oils, fuels and solvents).

☑ The illegal burning of waste materials and fly tipping.

☑ The build up of hazardous substances or waste materials, resulting in them being washed into the ground by rainwater.

☑ Failing to adequately protect waste material skips, resulting in rainwater washing harmful residues out.

☑ The poor planning or lack of supervision of work activities, which can allow unsuitable actions or affect the quality of life of other people.

☑ The poor maintenance of plant and equipment allowing excessive noise or air pollution.

E
18

 A spill involving just one litre of oil can contaminate one million litres of drinking water.

Your part in preventing pollution

To avoid creating pollution you should always adhere to the following.

Spill kit deployed

☑ Follow the instructions in the COSHH assessment and any site rules when using any substance, particularly with regard to storage and disposal.

☑ Keep oils, fuels and chemicals within bunded areas when not in use.

☑ Keep the lids on tins of paints, adhesives and solvents when not in use.

☑ Prevent spillages, particularly into open ground, by careful handling and decanting of harmful liquids.

☑ Keep harmful substances at least 10 m away from watercourses, drains, and so on.

☑ Minimise the waste of materials by storing anything that can be rain-damaged under cover.

✋ **Pollution spreads easily**

Spilt or leaking oils, including fuel, can be particularly damaging to the environment.

It is possible for spilt or leaking substances to soak deep into the ground and pollute groundwater, which in some cases becomes domestic drinking water.

5 litres of oil can contaminate an area **the size of two football pitches.**

If it gets into the **groundwater,** pollution may appear **several miles away.**

 Spilt materials must be properly contained using absorbent materials, not washed down with detergent.

E 18

When refuelling site vehicles or construction plant, this must be carried out in an area with a hard surface that prevents spilt fuel from soaking into the ground. The following points should be implemented if refuelling has to be carried out away from these areas, where the ground is unprotected.

☑ A drip tray must be used (this must be cleared of any spilt fuel afterwards by using absorbent spill clean-up materials).

☑ Refuelling must take place at least 10 m from watercourses or drains. (Where 10 m cannot be achieved speak with your supervisor who should then put in place further control measures.)

 Regulatory bodies recommend that refuelling is always carried out under supervision.

Where possible, refuelling should be carried out using a pumped system through a nozzle fitted with an automatic cut-off to prevent over-filling and therefore spillages. Where necessary, funnels should be used to assist in preventing spills.

Do not dispose of harmful substances into drains or gullies. Site drain covers should be colour coded to show what is allowed to pass through the drain.

Blue	Surface water (such as clean, uncontaminated rainwater).
Red	Foul water (such as sewage and silty run-off water).
Red 'C'	Combined surface and foul water.

If the product you are using displays either of the following signs on the label or COSHH assessment then it is harmful to the environment. Anything left over, including the container, must be disposed of in line with the label or site rules.

Ground that was used or built on before may contain hazardous substances. You must immediately **stop** and tell your supervisor if you find either of the following.

☑ Soil that has a strange smell and/or appears to be oily.

☑ Fragments or clumps of fibres that could be asbestos or other hazardous materials.

If you are involved in pumping water out of an excavation (de-watering) you must be aware that silty water must be treated before it can be discharged into surface water drains or ditches. Site management or your supervisor must make the decision upon whether the water is silty.

Pollution incidents

 If you are aware that an environmental incident or spill has occurred then act quickly and follow these simple steps: stop – contain – notify.

☑ **Stop** work immediately and prevent any more substance spilling (such as right an oil drum or close a valve).

☑ **Eliminate** any sources of ignition (for example, switch off plant).

☑ **Assess** the situation. Make sure you have the right personal protective equipment (PPE) and wait for help if this is needed. Do not put yourself at risk.

☑ **Contain** the spill using a spill kit or by building earth or sand bunds immediately.

E
18

☑ **Check** the spill has not reached any nearby drains, manholes, watercourses, ditches, ponds or other sensitive areas.

☑ **Cover** drains or manholes to stop the substance entering the drainage system.

☑ **Notify** your supervisor or employer of an incident as soon as possible.

☑ **Dispose** of all contaminated materials (such as absorbent granules, soil or cleaning cloths) used to contain a spill in the correct hazardous waste skip.

 Report the facts to your supervisor or employer, who should notify the Environment Agency (in England) or Natural Resources Wales (in Wales), by the emergency hotline: 0800 80 70 60.

Waste materials

Environmental damage can result from waste materials in the following circumstances.

☑ If it is allowed to accumulate and is not protected from the weather and scavenging animals.

☑ Where hazardous waste is mixed with other waste (such as asbestos cement mixed with rubble).

☑ If it is illegally disposed of or fly-tipped.

 Everyone on site has a part to play in preventing environmental damage by being aware of the potential environmental risks that arise from their work.

You have a responsibility to identify how and where you create waste so that efforts can be made to cut the amount produced. Always check if someone else can use what you are about to throw away as it might have a use elsewhere.

Segregated waste bins

Different types of waste should be segregated into different skips so that they can be recycled more easily. Recycling waste means that it does not have to go to landfill.

To assist, colour coded labels are put on skips to show what type of waste should be put in them. *(Refer to the table on the following page.)*

E
18

Label colour	Waste
Blue	Metallic
Green	Wood and timber
White	Gypsum and plaster
Orange	Hazardous
Brown	Packaging
Grey	Inert
Black	Mixed non-hazardous
Red	Asbestos
Yellow	Clinical

 Hazardous waste must never be mixed in with other types of waste.

If hazardous waste gets into landfill it can be damaging to the environment.

Examples of hazardous waste

☑ Asbestos.

☑ Batteries.

☑ Used spill kits.

☑ Fluorescent light tubes.

☑ Waste solvents (such as white spirit, oil and bitumen based paints).

☑ Epoxy resins and mastics.

Oily rags segregated into hazardous waste containers

E
18

Nuisance

No-one on site, or off it, should have to suffer nuisance and possibly ill health because of site activities.

If you think that your work might be a nuisance to other people (for example, as per the items listed below) you should report it to your supervisor.

Managing dust and emissions

☑ Causing too much noise, particularly during unsocial hours.

☑ Creating vibration that can be felt off site.

☑ Generating smoke.

☑ Vehicle fumes being a nuisance to nearby properties or people.

☑ Creating off-site dust clouds from haul roads.

☑ Site lighting or task lights shining onto nearby properties or people, including road traffic.

☑ Mud or dust being deposited on public roads or footpaths.

E
18

19

Demolition

What your site and employer should do for you

1. Provide you with a written method of working that is safe and without risks to your health (demolition plan or demolition task sheets).

2. Make sure that a competent person supervises the work, where necessary.

3. Tell you about the significant hazards identified in the risk assessment.

4. Explain the safe way of working to you, which will be in a method statement.

5. At no time place you in danger.

6. Provide you with adequate PPE, RPE instruction and training.

What you should do for your site and employer

1. Follow the agreed safe system of work.

2. Not take risks with your own or anyone else's health or safety.

3. Report any aspect of your work that you feel is unsafe or a threat to health.

4. Comply with any permit systems that are in operation.

F
19

Introduction

Demolition is a highly specialised and potentially dangerous activity. Health and safety law requires that it is only carried out by trained and competent demolition contractors.

☑ A competent person must be appointed to supervise the work before it starts.

☑ Before starting any demolition project, the risk assessment must be inspected to identify the intended way of controlling the hazards.

Planning the work

The demolition contractor must make sure that the work is planned and carried out in such a way that it avoids danger or, where this is not possible, reduces the danger as far as is reasonably practicable. This will include the following requirements.

☑ Recording the arrangements for health and safety in writing before the work starts.

☑ Identifying, locating and isolating all services.

☑ Identifying the location of any asbestos through a refurbishment or demolition survey carried out before work starts, by a trained and competent asbestos surveyor.

☑ Identifying any other hazardous materials or substances and planning their removal.

☑ Laying out the sequence of operations in a written demolition plan and ensuring that it is read out during site induction and understood by all involved.

Safe methods of working

Given the potentially hazardous nature of demolition work, it is essential that safe methods of work are developed and followed.

☑ If demolishing internal brick walls, you must work across in even courses, from the ceiling down.

☑ The electricity company must be consulted if work has to be carried out near to overhead cables.

☑ If underground services that were not identified earlier are discovered, work must stop until the situation has been resolved.

☑ A gas-free certificate must be obtained before carrying out the demolition cutting of any fuel tank.

☑ Gas free certificates are only valid for 24 hours after being issued.

☑ Make sure the site is secure to prevent unauthorised access, particularly by children outside of working hours.

☑ Make sure there is enough clear signage (for example indicating the boundary of exclusion zones).

☑ Work at height must be avoided where possible. Where such work must be carried out, it should be carefully planned and carried out to prevent the fall of people or materials.

F
19

☑ Do not allow combustible waste materials (demolition soft strip materials arising from the works) to accumulate.

Health hazards

Due to the nature of the working environment demolition can present some potentially serious, long-term threats to the health of the people involved if the risks are not controlled. Health issues are often overlooked because of the long-term nature of some diseases.

☑ Where asbestos is found to be present it must be removed, as far as is reasonably practicable, before the job starts.

☑ If, during demolition, it is suspected that some asbestos-containing material or lead (for example old painted steelwork) remains in the structure, work must stop immediately and a supervisor must be told.

☑ Lead-based paint might be present under asbestos clad or coated steelwork.

☑ If you have come into contact with lead you must wash your hands and face before eating or drinking.

☑ If you have been involved in the hot cutting of coated steel you must be aware of the potential for exposure to harmful levels of lead in the blood.

☑ COSHH assessments must cover any other harmful substances likely to be released.

☑ The safe system of work must prevent exposure to hand-arm vibration through the use of equipment (such as breakers or drills).

☑ Exposure to too much vibration in your hands and arms can lead to vibration white finger.

☑ Demolition is likely to release airborne dust (such as silica). (The need for respiratory protective equipment (RPE) is covered later in this section.)

☑ Skin diseases (such as dermatitis) must be prevented by ensuring there is no skin contact with harmful substances.

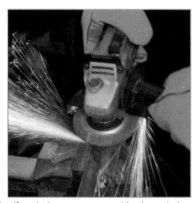

Examples of tools that could cause hand-arm vibration if control measures are not implemented

F
19

Personal protective equipment

Wearing the correct personal protective equipment (PPE) can prevent exposure to harmful substances; the wrong type of PPE is likely to be useless. The person in charge of the site must make sure that where necessary the correct PPE is worn, as in the situations below, for example.

☑ Higher grade RPE than might be necessary for work (a minimum of an FFP3 facemask with suitable filter, depending upon the protection factor required).

☑ A positive pressure-powered respirator, a compressed airline breathing apparatus or self-contained breathing apparatus is needed if working in a dusty atmosphere.

Note: a half-mask dust respirator may not provide the necessary level of protection.

☑ A positive pressure-powered respirator or a ventilated respirator is provided when cutting coated steelwork.

Plant and equipment

Anyone who has to operate any item of plant or equipment (for example a MEWP) must be trained, competent and authorised.

☑ Information on the daily checks for mobile plant can be found:
  – on stickers attached to the machine
  – in the manufacturer's handbook
  – in information provided by the supplier of the machine.

☑ The extent of the daily checks that must be carried out by the operator include checking the emergency systems, engine oil and hydraulic fluid levels.

☑ Operators must never try to move a machine if they do not have adequate visibility from the driving position (such as losing sight of the vehicle marshaller).

☑ Unattended mobile plant must be left in a safe place with the keys removed and the doors locked.

☑ The head and tail lights of any machine must be switched on when the plant is operating in all conditions of poor visibility.

☑ An item of plant that is defective must be isolated so that no-one else can try to use it and its condition must be reported.

☑ Machines that operate in areas where there may be falling materials must be fitted with a falling object protective structure (FOPS).

☑ Roll-over protective structures (ROPS) must be fitted to plant to protect the driver where there is a danger of it rolling over.

☑ Operators must face the machine when climbing down from it.

☑ Passengers must only be carried on construction plant if a purpose-made passenger seat is fitted.

☑ All plant must be inspected, with the details recorded, at least every week.

F
19

☑ Plant movements and traffic routes must be planned and co-ordinated to make sure:
- there is no conflict between different types of vehicles
- pedestrians are safe
- the movement of materials is safe
- there is safe access to and egress from the site.

Lifting operations

Poorly thought out lifting operations and defective equipment have been the cause of many accidents.

☑ A method statement (lifting plan) must be drawn up for all lifting operations.

☑ Anyone not involved in lifting operations should be kept out of the area.

☑ Lifting equipment that is **not** used for lifting people must be thoroughly examined at least every 12 months.

☑ Lifting accessories (such as chains, shackles, slings and strops) and equipment used for lifting people must be thoroughly examined every six months.

☑ If any lifting accessory is found to be defective it must not be used and must be isolated so that no-one can try to use it.

☑ All lifting operations must be carried out within the safe working load (SWL) of any item of lifting equipment and any lifting accessories used.

☑ The SWL must be marked upon each item of lifting equipment and each lifting accessory.

Confined spaces

Working in confined spaces is well known as a potentially hazardous activity. Many people have died through lack of planning or trying to rescue others.

☑ Before anyone starts working in a confined space they should be briefed on the risk assessment.

☑ During confined space working it is essential that the people doing the work strictly follow the conditions given in the permit to work.

☑ Before entering any open-topped tank a permit to work must be obtained.

☑ Carbon dioxide extinguishers must never be taken into a confined space as they contain a gas that is not breathable by human beings.

F
19

LPG, other gases and substances

By the nature of demolition activities, it is most likely that highly flammable and explosive substances will be stored and used on site at some time.

☑ It is essential that gases are stored a safe distance away from other gases, (for example oxygen cylinders must be stored more than 3 m away from LPG cylinders).

☑ LPG cylinders that are used for heating or cooking in a site cabin must be stored outside the cabin.

☑ The correct type of fire extinguishers must be available where petrol or diesel are being stored. Water extinguishers must **not** be provided.

☑ Flashback arrestors must be fitted between the pipes and gauges when using oxy-propane cutting equipment.

☑ Cans or drums of fluids must be stored in bunded areas to prevent any leaks from spreading.

☑ If unlabelled drums or containers are discovered, work must stop until they have been safely dealt with.

LPG store

F
19

Demolition

20

Highway works

What your site and employer should do for you

1. Develop safe methods that offer you maximum protection from road users and hazards.

2. Train you if you work on any live highway.

3. Train you if you operate mobile plant or equipment.

4. Provide, maintain and inspect the correct plant and equipment.

5. Provide the correct PPE for tasks and high-visibility clothing for the road type.

What you should do for your site and employer

1. Follow the step-by-step safe system of work and site or highway traffic rules.

2. Position signs and cones in the right sequence and in the correct place.

3. Wear your task specific PPE (high-visibility clothing, seat belts, and so on) at all times.

4. Do not work in the safety zone and do not use hand signals to control traffic.

5. Report any defects and complete any required daily and weekly inspections.

F
20

Signing, lighting and guarding

The working environment on the highway will involve you working with, or alongside, pedestrians and moving traffic and will lead to problems rising from confusion, conflict and delays.

To reduce this, a clear and concise **signing, lighting and guarding** procedure must be put in place.

Temporary traffic management (TTM) forms the basis of warning, informing and directing the pedestrian and the road user, through and round the site, by the means of signs, cones, and barriers. Most of the common situations are described in the Code of Practice *(Safety at Street Works and Road Works) – the Red book.* Further advice can be found in Chapter 8 of the *Traffic signs manual.*

Safe works – basic principles

☑ To comply with health and safety legislation, a safe system of work will need to be in place to make sure that a risk assessment, in respect to signing, lighting and guarding, is completed.

☑ It is your responsibility to sign, guard, light and maintain your works safely.

☑ It is management's responsibility to provide equipment in good condition – it is your responsibility to use it in the correct way.

☑ You will need to wear high-visibility clothing whether visiting or working on the site.

☑ Signs, lights and guarding equipment should be secured by bags of granular material placed at low level, to avoid them being moved by wind or passing traffic.

☑ Check regularly, at least once every day, that signs and cones have not been moved, and have not become damaged or dirty.

☑ Drivers must be able to see the advance warning signs. Where visibility is poor, or there are obstructions, extra signs should be provided. Signs should be set out for traffic approaching from all possible directions.

☑ You may have to duplicate warning signs on both sides of the road (for example where signs on the left-hand side are obscured by heavy traffic).

☑ You must include the works area, working space and safety zone in the area to be marked off with cones (and lamps if necessary). Never use a safety zone as a work or storage area.

☑ If there are temporary footways in the carriageway, or obstructions (such as stored materials or plant, not already within the working space), sign and guard them separately to the same standard.

☑ In many cases traffic control will be necessary.

☑ Traffic conditions may change from those expected and alterations may be needed. If in doubt consult your supervisor.

☑ On finishing the work make sure that all plant, equipment and materials are removed quickly from the site. All signs, lighting and guarding equipment must be removed immediately when they are no longer needed – it is a legal requirement.

F
20

Site layout

The site layout consists of the following.

☑ Advance signing – length depends on the speed and type of road.

☑ Works area.

☑ Working space.

☑ Safety zone, including the following.
  - Lead-in taper.
  - Longways clearance.
  - Sideways clearance.
  - Exit taper.

Setting out signs

The safety zone is provided to protect you from the traffic and to protect the traffic from you. You may only enter it to maintain cones and other road signs. Materials and equipment must not be placed in it. The sideways clearance is the space between the working space and the moving traffic and varies with the speed limit. If pedestrians are diverted into the carriageway, you must provide a safety zone between the outer pedestrian barrier and the traffic. If the carriageway width does not permit the full sideways clearance you must consult your supervisor. It may be necessary to divert traffic or reduce speeds to below 10 mph.

 Don't work in the safety zone – you may lose more than your hat.

Setting out the site

You are at greatest risk when setting out the site, so make sure the following precautions are in place.

F
20

☑ Switch on your flashing beacon(s).

☑ Stop the vehicle in a safe place.

☑ Put on your high-visibility clothing.

☑ Get out of the vehicle on the passenger side where possible.

☑ Observe traffic movement at all times.

☑ Position signs in the correct sequence, at the correct distance and where they can be seen clearly – they must not cause a hazard to pedestrians.

☑ Secure the signs with sandbags.

☑ Check that all of the signs are correct before starting work.

Other considerations

Pedestrian movement

Footway working may mean the re-routing of pedestrians. You may need to provide a temporary footway, minimum width as in the Code of Practice, using barriers (with tapping rails for the blind or partially sighted), ramps and information signs.

Footpath diversion showing the safe pedestrian route

Works vehicles

All works vehicles should be of a conspicuous colour and must have an amber warning beacon. Any vehicle entering a site must switch on the amber beacon. This reduces the risk of having been followed into the site by private vehicles; should this occur you will need to assist the driver to leave the site via the nearest safe designated exit.

Motorways and high speed dual carriageways (50 mph and above)

Extra precautions are necessary, including the following.

☑ Long sleeved high-visibility clothing must be worn.

☑ Advance warning signs need to be duplicated on the central reservation.

☑ All traffic management must be undertaken by a registered traffic management contractor.

☑ If you are entering a site on a motorway, you must switch on your flashing amber beacon and the correct indicator about 200 m before the access point, to give following traffic enough advance warning.

F
20

Short stop/mobile working operations

These include continuous mobile operations (such as hedge trimming), as well as those which involve movement with periodic stops (for example gully emptying) and short duration works (for example pothole filling). This work must only be carried out where there is good visibility and during periods of low risk (such as light traffic).

The basic requirements for the works vehicle are listed below.

☑ It must be conspicuously coloured.

☑ It must have one or more roof-mounted amber flashing beacons operating.

☑ A keep right/left arrow sign must be displayed on or at the rear of the vehicle, showing drivers approaching on the same side of the carriageway which side to pass. This directional sign must be covered or removed when travelling to and from the site.

This is the minimum traffic management needed for short stop/mobile operations.

Advance warning signs are necessary when there is not enough space for two-way traffic to pass the works vehicle or where it cannot be seen clearly. The signs should be placed up to one mile from the works vehicle.

Traffic control systems

Under no circumstances should you use hand signals to control traffic. Only the police are legally allowed to do this.

 The *Red book* describes the various systems, where and when they may be installed, and should be consulted in all cases.

Give and take

☑ Speed limit 30 mph or less.

☑ Coned off area 50 m or less.

☑ Drivers approaching the works can see at least 50 m beyond the end of the works.

☑ Traffic, including heavy goods vehicles, is light.

Priority signs

☑ Coned off area 80 m or less.

☑ Drivers approaching the works can see at least 60 m beyond the end of the coned area for 30 mph speed limit. Other distances are given for different speed limits.

☑ Two-way traffic flow is light.

Stop/go boards

☑ Works length can be up to 500 m depending on two-way traffic flow levels.

☑ Normally use stop/go boards at each end of the works.

F
20

☑ Where visibility is impeded, a communication system must be employed.

☑ Allow enough time for traffic to clear with both boards showing 'stop'.

☑ Consult your supervisor if the works are near a railway level crossing or a road junction.

Portable traffic signals (temporary traffic lights)

☑ Works length can normally be up to 300 m.

☑ Signals must be put up and removed in an organised way and specific sequence.

☑ Allow more time for slow-moving traffic, cyclists and horse riders, by increasing the all-red timings.

☑ Most sites will only need one set of signal heads. Where visibility is poor a double-headed system should be used.

☑ Where signal cables cross the carriageway, cable protectors must be used and the signs ramp/ramp ahead must be used.

☑ If the detector systems become faulty, you must operate the signals on fixed time or manually, and contact the service company or your supervisor.

Mobile plant

Maintaining mobile plant

If you are an operator you are responsible for daily and weekly maintenance to make sure your plant and/or equipment is in a safe condition, giving particular attention to the following.

Operative being trained on pre-use checks

☑ Maintaining correct tyre pressure, as failure could lead to instability and increased or uneven tyre wear.

☑ Ensuring the horn, flashing beacon, lights and indicators all work.

☑ Keeping windows and mirrors clean and mirrors adjusted for good visibility. This is particularly important when manoeuvring.

☑ Making sure windscreen wipers and washers operate efficiently, including keeping the washer bottle topped up.

☑ Checking levels of fuel, oil, water and brake fluids.

☑ Making sure brakes, including hand/parking brakes, operate efficiently and where air brakes are fitted the air storage tanks must be drained daily.

☑ Keeping the cab clean, tidy and clear of any loose articles that may obstruct the operation of foot pedals and controls.

☑ Checking that your clothing, especially if you are a wearing a winter jacket, does not snag on controls/dead man switches.

**F
20**

Diesel must never be used to clean mobile plant or prevent bitumen or asphalt sticking to buckets or load beds, as this will make it slippery and present a serious risk of injury from slips and falls. Use suitable access equipment to prevent serious injury from falls when hosing down plant, especially for high level or load beds of lorries and gritters.

 Mobile plant in an unsafe condition must not be used.

Operating mobile plant

If you operate plant you must be trained/competent to operate the type of plant you are authorised to use. You should have a suitable driving licence and/or plant operator's certificate/card. Before operating any plant for the first time, you should read and understand the manufacturer's operating instructions and be familiar with the controls and their function.

- ☑ You must not work too many hours (the Drivers' Hours Regulations and Working Time Regulations limit the number of hours that may be worked in any day or week).

- ☑ Operator and plant record books must be completed where necessary.

- ☑ You must be aware of the gross vehicle weight, the maximum axle weights and overall dimensions of the plant.

- ☑ When refuelling any plant, remember, no smoking or naked lights and switch off the ignition.

- ☑ You are responsible for the safe operation and condition of your mobile plant at all times.

- ☑ You must comply with road traffic legislation and site rules where applicable.

- ☑ The use of an amber beacon does not exempt you from compliance with the Highway Code.

- ☑ You must stop operations immediately and report defects that present a serious risk to the safe operation of plant (such as faulty controls or 'dead man's handle').

- ☑ Where fitted, seatbelts must be worn (they could save your life).

- ☑ Use mirrors and CCTV, if fitted, when manoeuvring.

- ☑ A vehicle marshaller must be used when reversing in areas where there may be pedestrians.

- ☑ Do not operate mobile plant too close to any excavation, no matter how shallow. Stop blocks are the preferred method of preventing mobile plant getting too near to an excavation when tipping.

- ☑ Obey all speed limit, height restriction, direction and warning signage.

- ☑ Be alert to the dangers of colliding with or clipping scaffolding, temporary works, mobile towers, mobile elevating work platforms (MEWP) and ladders.

Parking

- ☑ Where possible, park on level ground in a designated area, clear of pedestrians. Handbrake/parking brake should be on, engine off and key removed.

- ☑ If you cannot park on level ground you may need to chock the wheels or otherwise prevent unintended movement of the plant.

F 20

☑ All hydraulic equipment (such as buckets, forks and back-actors) should be lowered to the rest position.

Access

☑ Only authorised people should be allowed onto mobile plant.

☑ Passengers may only be carried on mobile plant equipped with sufficient, suitable seating for them.

☑ Wait until the mobile plant has come to a complete stop before getting on and off. Never jump down – always use the steps and grab rails.

☑ Maintain three points of contact with access ladders or hand/foot holds.

☑ Never, at any time, work under an unpropped mobile plant body.

 Maintain three points of contact – don't jump down.

The following operations may need detailed consideration and risk assessment to work out safe access.

☑ Sheeting loads.

☑ Maintenance.

☑ Working at height at the top of the mobile plant.

☑ Anywhere else where falls may be likely.

Loads

Loading and the load are the operator's responsibility.

☑ Plant must not be overloaded and loads must be spread evenly and secured.

☑ Operators of mobile plant should not remain in the seat or unprotected cab while it is being mechanically loaded.

☑ Check sideboards, curtains, sheeting and tailboards are fastened and secure before moving off.

☑ Check load for security. Any projections must be properly marked and clearly visible.

☑ Care should be taken when removing lashings as the load may have shifted during transit or moved when being released.

☑ Loading and unloading of tippers must be attended by a competent vehicle marshaller. Rear end tippers are liable to overturn whilst tipping on uneven or made up ground.

☑ People should stay well clear of any tipping or loading operations.

☑ Tippers and dumpers must not travel with the body in the raised position after the load has been discharged.

F
20

Trailers

Before towing any trailer or plant, you must make sure you have the correct class of driving licence. It is essential to make sure that the driver is licensed for the specific combination (towing vehicle plus trailer and load).

☑ The towing vehicle, trailer and compressor must be compatible and any conversions secured with the correct towing pin.

☑ When being towed on a highway the trailer must be fitted with registration number plates and rear tail lights.

☑ Where fitted, trailer parking brakes must be applied before disconnecting the trailer from the towing vehicle. On slopes, trailer wheels should also be chocked.

☑ Trailers fitted with independent operating brakes should be connected to the towing vehicle by a cable, which will activate the trailer's brakes if the tow hitch fails. Otherwise the trailer must be fitted with a safety chain connected to the vehicle.

 Ratchet straps or similar should not be secured and tightened onto rope hooks, which have no safe working load. Only use designated securing points.

Mobile plant used for lifting

☑ Only authorised and trained operators should operate lifting equipment.

☑ All lifting operations should be properly planned by a competent person.

☑ Lifting equipment should get a daily visual check before use.

☑ Lifting equipment must be subject to a recorded weekly inspection.

☑ Lifting accessories (chains, strops and shackles) must be thoroughly examined every six months.

All lifting operations should be properly planned

☑ Equipment for lifting people (such as a MEWP) must be thoroughly examined every six months.

☑ Other lifting equipment must be thoroughly examined every 12 months.

☑ Care must always be taken when operating extending booms or other lifting equipment near overhead power lines.

☑ The safest method is limiting the boom extension or height of the mast.

 The rated safe working load (SWL) of any lifting equipment must never be exceeded.

21

Specialist work at height

What your site and employer should do for you

1. Make sure work at height is properly planned so that your place of work at height and the access route to and from it are safe to occupy.

2. Provide, inspect and maintain the most suitable work at height equipment.

3. Provide adequate safety equipment to prevent falls, or if necessary to arrest any falls.

4. Make sure you are trained and regularly updated in methods of working safely at height.

5. Give you a written safe system of work which you fully understand so that you can work at height safely.

What you should do for your site and employer

1. Fully understand and follow the agreed safe system of work (including using any equipment provided to prevent or arrest falls).

2. Report any aspect of your work that you feel is unsafe.

3. Not interfere with anything provided for safety unless you are trained, competent and authorised.

4. Not use powered access equipment if you have not been trained.

5. Not take risks or short cuts.

6. Report any falls which occur, even if they cause no injury.

F
21

Introduction

☑ Every year many deaths and serious injuries result from falls from height.

☑ All too often the same types of accidents reoccur (such as falls through fragile roof materials and falls from ladders).

☑ In many cases taking basic safety precautions and/or providing training could have prevented suffering.

The likelihood of an injury as a result of working at height can be increased if you are regularly in this situation.

 You should also read Chapter D16 Working at height, which explains what employers and in some cases you must do to comply with the law and keep yourself, and others, safe whilst working at height.

Safe working at height

Safely working at height depends upon the following.

☑ The work being properly planned with a safe system of work in place, which follows the hierarchy of control for working at height.

☑ The people who will carry out the job being adequately trained, competent and authorised.

☑ The job being carried out in line with the safe system of work.

☑ The tools and equipment used have been inspected and maintained properly.

☑ Adequate supervision being provided, as necessary.

Before you starting working at height (for example on a roof) there are many things that your employer, or you, can do to make sure that the job is carried out safely. Some examples are shown below.

☑ Assessing the risks arising from the work and taking measures which will:
   – prevent people or materials falling from height
   – make sure that there are no serious injuries or damage if someone or something does fall.

☑ Drawing up a method statement that explains exactly how the job should be carried out and making sure that the people doing the job understand it. The method statement should include details of the following.
   – How falls will be prevented.
   – The sequence of operations that must be carried out.
   – The equipment to be used.
   – Who will supervise the job.

If you are not sure that what you have been asked to do is safe or you are unhappy about any other aspect of working at height, you should talk about it with your supervisor.

F
21

Generally, the risks will depend on the following.

Working at height in a safe environment

☑ How experienced the people are in doing the job they need to do.

☑ The number of people who will be working at height.

☑ The length of time that people will be working at height.

☑ The method of access chosen to get the people doing the job up to the workplace.

☑ The nature of the place of work (such as scaffold platform or leading edge of new roof).

☑ Whether or not precautions and a rescue plan are necessary in case something does fall.

☑ The weather.

☑ The nature of any materials that will have to be hoisted and/or stored at height.

☑ The method of hoisting materials.

☑ Whether or not people can be kept out of the area below where the work is taking place.

 Falls are still the biggest killer, but many could easily have been prevented.

F
21

Hierarchy for working at height

Any person planning work at height should always follow a hierarchy of control and consider options at the top of the hierarchy before moving down.

> **Step 1. Avoid working at height**
> **e.g. assemble on the ground and lift into position using a crane or by fixing guard-rails to structural steelwork on the ground before lifting and fixing at height.**

> **Step 2. Prevent falls from occurring**
> **Use an existing safe place of work**
> **e.g. parapet walls, defined access points, a flat roof with existing edge protection**

> **Step 3. Prevent falls through providing *collective* protection**
> **e.g. scaffolding, edge protection, handrails, podium steps, mobile towers, MEWPs**

> **Step 4. Prevent falls through providing *personal* protection**
> **e.g. using a work restraint (travel restriction) system that prevents a worker getting into a fall position**

> **Step 5. Minimise the distance and/or consequences of a fall using *collective* protection**
> **e.g. safety netting, airbags or soft-landing systems**

> **Step 6. Minimise the distance and/or consequences of a fall using *personal* protection (The last resort)**
> **e.g. industrial rope access (working on a building façade) or a fall-arrest system using a high anchor point**

F
21

Roof work

Much work that is carried out at height involves working on roofs, which can be hazardous.

☑ Fragile roofs are particularly dangerous because it is not always clear at the start whether or not the roof cladding is a fragile material. A safe system of work must be in place.

☑ If you have any doubts, you should check the risk assessment or method statement and speak to your supervisor.

☑ High-level features (such as overhead cables) present further danger.

☑ Surfaces are likely to become slippery after rain, frost, or snow.

☑ If you are working near power cables check with your supervisor or the person in charge of the site that it is safe to be on the roof.

☑ Fragile roof lights can be dangerous if not barriered-off or covered with securely fixed covers that can withstand any load imposed upon them.

☑ Specialist access equipment is likely to be needed for carrying out work above fragile roofs (for example the inspection of pipework).

☑ Materials must be stored on roofs in a safe way so that:

    – the pitch of the roof is taken into account when deciding what can be stored safely

    – they cannot fall or be blown off the roof

    – during loading-up an excessive 'point loading' is avoided

    – they are quickly distributed around the roof to where they are needed

    – a safe method of getting them up to the roof is employed (for example inclined hoist, scaffold-hoist, safety pulley or gin-wheel)

    – they do not pose a hazard to anyone working on the roof

    – they can be accessed safely.

If you are planning to use a roof ladder consider the following.

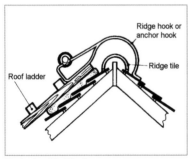

Ridge hook or anchor hook

Ridge tile

Roof ladder

Typical roof ladder in use

☑ It must be purpose made or a normal ladder fitted with a proprietary fitting.

☑ A stable working platform at eaves height will provide safe access to the roof ladder with the added feature of edge protection.

☑ If using a leaning ladder for access, the transition between ladders must be safe.

☑ A leaning ladder used for access must be stable and extend 1 m above eaves height.

☑ Whether a roof scaffold is a better option.

Fall prevention methods

Scaffolds

A common way of preventing falls is to use a secure and stable working platform (such as a scaffold). Below are some essential considerations when using scaffolds.

☑ Is it a safe and suitable means of access for the job that has to be done (for example are the lift heights satisfactory)?

☑ They must only be erected, altered and dismantled by a person who is trained and competent. The scaffolder should hold a current industry recognised CISRS card.

☑ Each working platform must be wide enough to allow the job to be carried out safely and for the passage of people and equipment as necessary.

☑ Never overload working platforms, as this has been the cause of many scaffold collapses.

☑ Anyone who is **not** trained, competent and authorised must never interfere with a scaffold, (for example by removing a tie or guard-rail which is in their way).

☑ Where someone could be injured by a fall from a working platform or hit by falling objects, edge protection must be fitted to the working platforms.

☑ Every scaffold must be inspected periodically by a competent person, with the findings of the inspection entered in a register. Details may also be recorded on a plastic tag, usually fixed to the scaffold next to the access point.

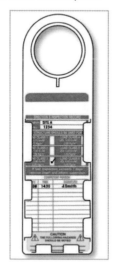

Typical scaffold tagging system

 If you notice any unauthorised modifications to a scaffold, report it to your supervisor straight away.

F
21

Mobile elevating work platform

Common types of mobile elevating work platform (MEWP) are cherry pickers (boom type) and scissor lifts. Safety considerations when using a MEWP are shown below.

Emergency descent symbol

Ref. IPAF D1

☑ You must not operate any type of MEWP unless you are trained, competent and authorised. Holding an IPAF card is a good indication.

☑ Users of cherry pickers must normally wear a safety harness and restraint (fixed-length) lanyard secured to the designated anchorage point.

☑ It must allow safe access to the place of work. If it does not reach, a larger machine is necessary. Do not stand on the guard-rails or put a stepladder or hop up on the working platform.

☑ The ground-level controls must only be used in an emergency (for example if the operator becomes ill or is trapped).

Note: if there is an emergency, a responsible person on the ground should know where to find and use the lowering controls (sometimes shown by an emergency descent symbol).

☑ There must be a rescue plan in place in case the operator is stuck or injured and cannot lower the working platform.

☑ Before elevating the machine, operators must identify any projections or other features on the structure which could trap them between the guard-rails and the structure.

☑ Operators must know how to carry out daily and weekly checks.

☑ A MEWP must not be used as a substitute for the stairs in the structure being worked on.

☑ The person planning the job must make sure that a survey is carried out to identify any overhead hazards or underground voids (such as drains or cellars) which could collapse under the load.

☑ Only use a MEWP in areas covered by your lift plan, as ground conditions may not have been assessed in other areas.

☑ Operators must be aware of the wind-loading on a raised MEWP and be prepared to stop work and lower the machine if the wind speed is judged to be too high.

☑ Wind speed forecasts should be obtained before work commences.

☑ The Beaufort Scale can provide both managers and workers with indicators of prevailing wind conditions. The scale categorises the wind strength between Force 0 and Force 9. The higher the number the higher the wind-speed (for example Force 2 is a light breeze and Force 7 is a near gale).

F
21

 Never carry more than the maximum safe load in a MEWP. The maximum load in kilogrammes or number of people will be shown in your lift plan and displayed on the machine.

Access towers

☑ Access towers can be mobile or static, depending if wheels are fitted.

☑ They can be built from tube and fitting scaffold components or more commonly prefabricated alloy frames which slot together.

Tube and fitting towers must only be erected, altered or dismantled by a trained and competent scaffolder (for example someone who holds a CISRS card).

Alloy towers must only be built, altered or dismantled, in line with the manufacturer's instructions, by someone who has been trained and is competent on that type of tower (for example someone who holds a PASMA card).

Listed below are some safety considerations when using a tower.

☑ The guard-rails and toe-boards must have been fitted before the tower is used.

☑ Some types of alloy towers have guard-rails that can be positioned before the working platform is accessed.

☑ The brakes must be on at all times when a mobile tower is in use.

Safe working on a mobile tower, with toe-boards and both guard-rails in position and wheels locked

☑ The ground or floor surface must be level and sufficiently firm to take the loading of the base plates (static) or wheels (mobile).

☑ A mobile tower must not be moved whilst anyone or any equipment is on the platform.

☑ Once the platform of a mobile tower has been occupied the trapdoor must be closed immediately to prevent anyone or anything falling through it.

☑ The working platform must only be accessed by using the built-in ladder (**never** climb up the outside of a tower or use a free-standing ladder).

☑ Provision must be made for the safe hoisting of tools and materials up onto the platform.

☑ Every tower must be inspected periodically by a trained, competent and authorised person, including an inspection after any event that is likely to have made it unsafe to use (such as impact by a vehicle or being subjected to severe wind or weather).

Ladders and stepladders

More stable items of access equipment are often now used for some jobs that, at one time, would have been carried out using a ladder or stepladder. However, they can still be used for access to places of work at height and for carrying out light work of short duration where the risk of a fall is low. A properly carried out risk assessment will show whether a ladder or stepladder is a suitable item of access equipment to use for any particular job.

F
21

Some items that must be considered if you are going to use a ladder or stepladder are listed below.

☑ Possible defects, including splits in the material (from which the equipment is manufactured), missing or distorted rungs or frayed, and broken or missing tie-cords.

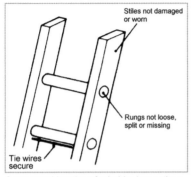

Stiles not damaged or worn

Rungs not loose, split or missing

Tie wires secure

Some considerations for ladder inspections

☑ Make sure that any ladder extends at least 1 m above the stepping-off point if there is not another handhold.

☑ Make sure that where a ladder is used for access to a high-level platform or similar, there is a landing at least every 9 m (about 30 foot) that the ladder rises vertically.

☑ Any ladder used on site must have been manufactured for heavy industrial use and it will be labelled 'Class 1'. Any ladder labelled 'Class 2' or 'BS EN 131' (light trade) or 'Class 3' (domestic use only) means that it is not suitable for use on a construction site.

☑ Various fittings (such as those below) are available that allow ladders to be used safely.
- Anti-slip mats and other anti-slip devices upon which the styles are positioned.
- Adjustable stabilisers to prevent sideways slipping.
- Adjustable extensions to allow use on sloping ground.
- Stand-off frames that avoid the need to rest ladders against fragile or flexible materials (such as plastic guttering).
- Ridge-hooks that allow an ordinary ladder to be converted to a roof ladder.

☑ Ladders are made from various materials.
- Generally alloy ladders are lighter than wooden ones but will conduct electricity and so cannot be used close to live overhead cables.
- Fibreglass ladders are non-conducting and so are safer to use near electrical supplies.

☑ If you are planning to use an extending ladder consider the following.
- Keep the minimum overlap between sections, as given in the manufacturer's instructions.
- The latching mechanism (and hoisting rope/fittings if appropriate) must be part of the pre-use inspection.
- The length/weight of the ladder and how many people will be raising it will decide whether it is safer to extend the ladder before raising it.
- Look for overhead obstructions **before** raising the ladder.

 All types of ladder will conduct electricity if they are wet.

F
21

Preventing falling objects

One of the obvious dangers of working at height is the possibility of materials, equipment, hand tools, and so on being dropped or thrown onto anyone below. Measures that should be taken to prevent this are listed below.

☑ Being aware of the presence of people, including the public, below the work area.

☑ Rigging a safety net, overlaid with a fine-mesh debris to prevent falling tools and materials from reaching the ground.

☑ Consider fitting a short lanyard with a wrist-loop to hand tools.

☑ Fitting edge protection to the working platforms of scaffolds.

☑ Wearing a chin-strap with a safety helmet to prevent it falling off if you need to bend over while working.

☑ Storing materials awaiting use in a safe way, away from the edges of flat roofs.

☑ Using a waste chute, with the bottom just above a skip, to move waste materials to a lower level.

Fall arrest (protecting you if you do fall)

Health and safety law recognises that there will be situations where physical barriers cannot be used, and the use of collective fall arrest measures (such as safety nets or airbags) is not practical. In these circumstances individual fall arrest measures (such as harness and lanyards) may be used as a **last resort**.

The following items should be considered when your employer chooses fall arrest measures.

☑ Collective fall arrest systems, (such as safety nets or airbags), which are preferable to personal protective measures (such as a harness and lanyard).

☑ A safety harness and lanyard should only be used in situations where:
   – it is not practical to use other fall arrest measures (such as a safety net or airbags)
   – a purpose-designed, secure anchor point is available (integral or mobile anchor)
   – users have been trained in the pre-use inspection, fitting and use of the equipment
   – users are aware that any damaged equipment must not be used
   – work must be planned to avoid a pendulum effect if someone does fall
   – a rescue plan is in place to reduce to a minimum the time that someone is suspended in a harness. A person's condition can deteriorate rapidly if they do not receive medical attention quickly.

☑ Essential features of any harness used for fall arrest are shown below.
   – It must be a full body harness that keeps someone who has fallen in an upright position until rescued.
   – Ideally it will be fitted with a feature that allows the person to raise their thighs above horizontal or to 'stand up' whilst awaiting rescue, releasing the pressure caused by the leg straps and reducing the chances of further injury.
   – It must be inspected before use, with more detailed inspections at periods set by the employer.

F
21

Safety nets

☑ Rig safety nets immediately below where people are working to minimise the height of any fall.

☑ Safety nets must only be rigged by someone who is trained, competent and authorised to do so.

☑ Work must stop if any damage to the net is discovered and the damage must be reported.

Safety nets installed prior to roof works commencing

☑ Materials or debris that have fallen into the net must be quickly cleared from it.

☑ No-one other than a trained and competent net rigger, should interfere with the securing cords. If you find one is in your way report the problem.

☑ Nets are often rigged using a MEWP, the floor surface must be suitable and able to withstand the loading.

☑ If a MEWP cannot be used it may be necessary to employ competent rope-access technicians to rig the nets (for example IRATA trained).

☑ Nets must be periodically inspected and any damaged nets replaced.

☑ Net repairs must only be carried out by a trained, competent and authorised person.

Airbags/bean bags

These systems can be an effective method of arresting falls, if they are installed correctly. They are generically known as *soft-landing systems*.

☑ They must be supplied and installed by competent contractors.

☑ They must be clipped together as necessary to provide a continuous fall protection area.

☑ Airbag inflation pumps must be kept running whenever anyone is working above them.

☑ They must fill the area over which fall arrest protection is needed.

☑ Airbags must not be too big; if over-size they will exert a sideways pressure on anything that is confining them as they inflate.

☑ Care must be taken to make sure that anyone who falls cannot bounce or slide onto another hazard (for example onto exposed rebar or out of a first floor window).

F
21

Rope access

☑ Rope access is a specialised activity requiring particular skills and training.

☑ Anyone engaged to carry out rope access must be IRATA (Industrial Rope Access Trade Association) or similar industry trained.

☑ Generally, rope access is needed where it is impractical to provide a working platform, other fall prevention methods or fall arrest measures.

☑ Tasks that rope access can be used for include the following.

- Structural surveys.
- Non-destructive testing.
- Localised concrete repairs.
- Cladding/glazing panel replacement.
- Secondary fixings.
- Surface preparation and decorating.
- Concrete spraying.
- Pressure pointing.

Rope access system
(Image supplied by PETZL)

F
21

F
21

22

Lifts and escalators

What your site and employer should do for you

1. Make sure that a competent person plans and supervises the work.

2. Provide you with a method of working that is safe and without risks to your health.

3. Explain the safe way of working to you, which will be in a method statement and risk assessment.

4. Provide you with the right tools and equipment for the job.

5. Provide you with adequate information, instruction and training.

What you should do for your site and employer

1. Follow the agreed safe system of work.

2. Use only equipment and methods you have been trained in.

3. Wear the right PPE for the task.

4. Not take risks or short cuts.

5. Stop and seek advice if anything changes or seems unsafe.

F
22

Overview and control measures

By the nature of the equipment, work on lifts and escalators can be hazardous and must only be taken on by trained, competent and authorised staff.

The actual requirements for this training and competence are detailed in Code of Practices BS 7255 *Safe working on lifts* and BS 7801 *Safe working on escalators and moving walks*.

The Lift and Escalator Industry Association (LEIA), which is responsible for the lift and escalator specialist section, represents most of the lift and escalator companies in the UK. Its members are committed to the LEIA safety charter, which requires member companies to work in line with BS 7255 and BS 7801.

Members should make sure, in particular, that all of their employees will undertake the following.

☑ Protect themselves and others from falls and falling objects.

☑ Use and verify **stop** and other devices when accessing, egressing and working on car tops and in lift and escalator pits to ensure total control of the equipment.

☑ Electrically isolate and lock off, when power is not needed and when working close to unguarded machinery.

These are just three essential control measures that must be implemented to ensure safe working.

For further guidance refer to:

**Lift and Escalator Industry Association
33–34 Devonshire Street
London
W1G 6PY**

**Tel: 020 7935 3013
Fax: 020 7935 3321**

www.leia.co.uk

**F
22**

Lifts and escalators

23

Tunnelling

What your site and employer should do for you

1. Make sure that a competent person plans and supervises the work.

2. Provide you with a method of working that is safe and without risks to your health.

3. Explain the safe way of working to you, which will be in a method statement and risk assessment.

4. Provide you with the right tools and equipment for the job.

5. Provide you with adequate information, instruction and training.

What you should do for your site and employer

1. Follow the agreed safe system of work.

2. Use only equipment and methods you have been trained in.

3. Wear the right PPE for the task.

4. Do not take risks or short cuts.

5. Stop and seek advice if anything changes or seems unsafe.

F
23

Introduction

Due to the nature of tunnelling, where people are often working far underground and a long way from a place of safety in the open air, the importance of working in a way which is safe and free of risks to health cannot be stressed enough.

The following text highlights some of the common potential hazards that could be experienced during tunnelling operations. The risk control measures and safe systems of work identified follow BS 6164, which is the Code of Practice for health and safety in tunnelling in the construction industry.

Safe systems of work

Formal safe systems of work are essential during tunnelling operations. Some examples are listed below.

☑ Ensuring continuous structural stability by immediately installing supports to excavated ground.

☑ Ensuring that where a shaft is being constructed, provision is made for:
- ventilation
- continuous gas monitoring
- adequate guarding.

☑ Using compressed air tunnelling, where necessary, to prevent or reduce the ingress of water during tunnel construction.

☑ Using water-spray curtains to help reduce the movement of smoke through a tunnel.

☑ Ensuring that personal protective equipment (PPE), safety signs and notices and a rescue plan are provided.

☑ Ensuring that the safe system of work for track maintenance workers and locomotive drivers, includes provision for the following.
- A lookout person.
- Flashing lights either side of the work area.
- Everyone involved in the job wearing high-visibility clothing.
- A permit to work.
- Adequate refuge points.

☑ Appreciating that falling objects or failure of the load is the greatest danger from suspended loads during shaft sinking operations.

☑ Storing tunnel segments in a secure way that prevents:
- falling or collapse
- any other movement
- instability.

A training tunnel
(© Crossrail Ltd)

F
23

☑ Protecting against the rebound or fall of materials during and after sprayed concrete operations.

☑ Taking great care to make sure that oxygen cylinders do not come into contact with grease, to avoid potential explosions.

☑ Wearing a safety harness when building rings from a platform within a shaft.

Communication

Effective communication is essential for safe tunnelling operations. For this reason, the power supply for communications equipment must be independent of the mains power supply so that it continues working if the mains power fails.

The most common form of communication between the surface and the tunnelling face is either by radio or a tannoy system.

You should **not** be allowed to work alone in tunnels because you may not be able to communicate with others if you have an accident or become unwell.

It is also important that you report any defects (such as damaged ventilation ducting) to a supervisor as soon as possible.

Safe access and egress

Safely getting to and from a place of work is equally as important as working safely whilst there.

Some things to consider are listed below.

☑ Fitting secure barriers of at least 1.2 m in height around every shaft, to prevent falls.

☑ Every working shaft must have a minimum of two escape methods or routes from each place where people are working.

☑ A tally system must be in place to control entry and exit to any tunnel under construction.

☑ Vertical ladders in tunnel shafts must have a landing (resting place) every 6 m.

☑ Safety nets and/or sliding doors must be fitted to man-riding cages/hoists/baskets to prevent anyone falling out or leaning out whilst they are in motion.

☑ Man-riding cages must not be overloaded. A label or notice will state the maximum number of people that can be carried.

☒ Water must not be allowed to accumulate above rail level in a tunnel for maintenance purposes.

Below are the **maximum** distances between safe refuges in a tunnel.

☑ 50 m – straight sections.

☑ 25 m – curved sections.

F
23

Emergency actions

In effect tunnels are confined spaces requiring, in most cases, that a self-rescue set is made available to each worker. Where one is provided, you should be aware of the following.

☑ It must be immediately available at all times.

☑ The duration of the air supply will be significantly reduced if you exert yourself whilst wearing it (such as when running).

☑ At best the air supply will only last for 20 minutes.

In an emergency the rescue services will use the tally-board to find out who is underground. A tally system counts people in and people out.

If there is an emergency or fire, if possible raise the alarm, and if safe to do so leave the tunnel.

If the ventilation system alarm activates you should immediately evacuate the workplace.

Fire and hot works

An underground fire can have devastating consequences. The close control of fire risks (such as those listed below) is therefore essential.

☑ Fire checks must be maintained for at least 60 minutes after hot works have ceased.

☒ Smoking, or even the carrying of smoking materials, is not permitted underground.

☒ Smoking or other naked flames are not permitted within **10 m** of battery charging areas because of the flammable gas produced by lead-acid batteries when they are charging.

☒ Hot works are not permitted within **10 m** of any diesel fuelling point.

Electrical safety

Emergency lighting, which must come on if the main lighting fails, must be installed in tunnels. The maximum distance between emergency lighting units is **50 m**.

For personal safety, apart from battery-operated tools, all powered hand tools must operate from a 110 volt supply.

Industrial electrical plugs and sockets are colour coded to show what voltage they are carrying.

Yellow	110 volt.
Blue	230 volt.
Red	400 volt.

F
23

Atmosphere

In tunnelling a safe, breathable atmosphere cannot always be guaranteed unless suitable control measures are taken.

Using the right equipment (as in the examples below) is essential to avoid hazards.

☑ Using intrinsically safe (spark proof) electrical and other equipment to prevent igniting potentially explosive atmospheres.

☑ Only using diesel-powered plant that is fitted with a **fixed** fire extinguishing system.

☒ **Not** using petrol-powered equipment at any time to avoid a lethal build-up of carbon monoxide.

Maintaining a satisfactory level of oxygen in the air is essential. Normally, there is 21% oxygen in the air we breathe. Oxygen deficiency, which causes breathlessness, occurs if the level falls below 19%.

There are potential dangers from other gases that may be found underground.

☑ Exposure to **hydrogen sulphide** can kill through respiratory paralysis. However it smells like rotten eggs and so its presence should be immediately obvious.

☑ **Methane** is explosive and it can displace the oxygen in the air, causing oxygen deficiency.

☑ Exposure to **carbon monoxide** prevents the intake of oxygen into the body.

☑ **Nitrogen oxide**, which is produced by diesel-powered equipment, can cause breathing problems.

 The use of a calibrated gas detector is a reliable way of detecting the presence of methane and carbon monoxide underground, if the risk of exposure cannot be eliminated.

Forced ventilation is one way of preventing the build up of hazardous gases underground. The failure of ventilation equipment must be indicated by an audible alarm and result in an immediate evacuation of the workplace.

Health risks

Tunnelling work will sometimes involve working in a compressed air environment. Decompression illness, often shortened to DCI, is a potential health risk.

Batching plants must be equipped with an eyewash station to provide quick treatment to anyone who has concrete splashed onto their face.

The following health risks are associated with sprayed concrete linings.

☑ Cement burns.

☑ Hand-arm vibration syndrome.

☑ Inhalation of dust.

**F
23**

The following health risks are associated with hand-mining.

☑ Hand-arm vibration syndrome.

☑ Noise.

☑ Inhalation of dust.

☑ Falling mined materials.

Hand-arm vibration syndrome can be caused by one or a combination of factors, the level of vibration and the exposure time. The effects, which include damage to the nerves and blood vessels in the hand, cannot be cured.

Equipment and moving plant

The movement or operation of plant in close proximity to where people are working will create a potentially dangerous situation unless a safe separation is maintained. Working in the confines of a tunnel can make this difficult to achieve. Below are some examples of good practice.

☑ Crush zones caused by moving plant will be indicated by:
  – signs or barriers
  – flashing warning lights.

☑ All conveyors must be fitted with:
  – an emergency stop system (pull cord or button)
  – an audible alarm to indicate that it is about to start.

☑ Inclined conveyors must be fitted with an anti roll-back device to prevent the belt running backwards due to power loss.

☑ Ensuring that segment erectors have a fail-safe device to stop the operation if the equipment experiences one of the following problems.
  – Suffers any malfunction.
  – Develops a leak.
  – Suffers a power supply failure.

☑ Fitting audible and/or visible alarms to rams and erectors of tunnel boring machines or hydraulic jacking rams in pipe-jacking shafts/pits, to warn when they are moving.

A student learning how to drive a tunnelling locomotive

☑ An additional control point is the most effective way of overcoming the restricted vision of tunnel boring machine (TBM) operators during the building process.

☑ Always using a hop up or refuge in a tunnel when vehicles are passing.

☑ Always go immediately to a hop up or refuge if a locomotive or other vehicle is approaching.

☑ The lights fitted to locomotives must be:
  – visible at a minimum distance of **60 m**
  – white (if fitted) to the front of the locomotive
  – red (if fitted) to the rear of the locomotive.

F
23

☑ Secondary couplings must be fitted to un-braked rolling stock to reduce the risk of it running away.

☑ In an emergency a locomotive must be able to stop with a distance not exceeding **60 m**.

☑ Ideally, the movement of locomotives when entering the back of a TBM will be controlled by:
- traffic lights
- closed circuit television (CCTV) in the cab.

☑ The traffic light system used to control plant movement underground is as follows.
- **Red** – stop.
- **Amber** – out bye.
- **Green** – in bye.

Pipework, services and hoses under pressure

All services running through the tunnel should be safely positioned to avoid them being damaged. The use of pressure systems is potentially hazardous unless safe work practices (such as those listed below) are adopted.

☑ Isolating or releasing stored energy before disconnecting or uncoupling tunnel services.

☑ Being aware that pumped grouting and sprayed concrete operations can result in the following.
- Injury resulting from burst hoses.
- Hearing damage and loss through exposure to excessive noise levels.
- Injury resulting from blowout at the injection point.

☑ Immediately releasing the pressure if a grouting or sprayed concrete hose becomes blocked.

☑ Cleaning grouting pipelines after use to prevent blockages and bursting when they are used again.

☑ Replacing hoses that show signs of swelling, which suggests they are damaged.

☑ Fitting anti-whip devices across flexible hose connections to prevent the ends flying about if they become disconnected under pressure.

☑ Including isolation arrangements in the safe system of work for maintenance work on grouting or slurry lines, especially if removing guards.

☑ Being aware that hoses, which are of a similar size but with different markings, are **not** interchangeable. Although hoses may appear similar, they may have one of the following attributes.
- Be of different physical sizes.
- Have different operating capacities.
- Be for different uses.

F
23

24

Heating, ventilation, air conditioning and refrigeration (HVACR)

What your site and employer should do for you

1. Provide you with a method of working that is safe and without risks to your health.

2. Make sure that a competent person will supervise the work.

3. Tell you about the significant hazards identified in the risk assessment.

4. Explain the safe way of working to you, which will be in a method statement.

5. At no time expect you to work unsafely or work in a place of danger.

6. Provide you with adequate instruction and training.

What you should do for your site and employer

1. Follow the agreed safe system of work.

2. Not take risks with your own or anyone else's health or safety.

3. Report any aspect of your work which you feel is unsafe.

4. Comply with any permit systems that are in operation.

F
24

Introduction

Common heating, ventilation, air conditioning and refrigeration (HVACR) elements below should be read by people from the following trades.

☑ Domestic heating and plumbing services (HAPS).

☑ Pipefitting and welding (industrial and commercial) (PFW).

☑ Ductwork (DUCT).

☑ Refrigeration and air conditioning (RAAC).

☑ Services and facilities maintenance (SAF).

You should also read the section later in the chapter that refers to your particular trade.

Common HVACR elements

Competency

Competency is essential if work is to be carried out in a way which is safe and free of risks to health. Competency can be defined as a combination of skills, training, attitude, knowledge and experience.

Competency is a 'two-way street'.

☑ No-one should ask any other person to carry out a job unless they are known to be competent to carry it out in a way that is safe and without risks to health.

☑ No person should be prepared to accept any job unless they know that they are competent to carry it out in a way that is safe and without risks to health.

Examples of good practice are listed below.

☑ All work must be properly planned in advance, with the risks assessed and eliminated or controlled.

☑ Only Gas Safe registered engineers are authorised to work on gas pipework or components.

☑ Dangerous gas fittings that could cause a death or major injury must be reported to the Health and Safety Executive.

☑ The pressure testing of pipework and vessels must only be carried out by someone who has been trained and is competent.

☑ All power tools must be used in a safe and responsible way.

☑ Only competent, trained people who work for an F-gas registered company are allowed to install, service or maintain systems that contain or are designed to contain refrigerant gases.

☑ Anyone who is concerned over their or anyone else's health or safety must report it to someone in authority on the site.

☒ The side of a cutting-off disc must **never** be used for grinding and anyone doing so must be stopped immediately.

F
24

Hot work

Hot work presents the obvious risk of fires on site unless the risks are managed; many serious fires have occurred on sites because they were not. For example, anyone carrying out hot work that involves the use of a blowtorch must make sure of the following.

☑ A fire extinguisher of the correct type is available in the immediate area.

☑ Remove lagging from pipework for at least 1 m either side of where work will be carried out on lagged pipes.

☑ Stop any work involving the use of a blowtorch at least one hour before leaving the job and inspect the area before leaving.

☑ Use a mat of a non-combustible material when a blowtorch is used near to any combustible materials (such as timber).

Anyone planning hot works must implement a hot work permit scheme and make sure it is followed.

Checking, installing, testing and commissioning installations

☑ Plant and equipment must be installed, tested and commissioned in such a way that it is safe to use.

☑ It is essential that the unauthorised use of plant and equipment is prevented, if necessary by the locking off of switches and valves, until such time as it has been fully commissioned.

Confined spaces and risers

Confined space working is recognised as being particularly hazardous.

☑ No-one should enter a confined space unless:
  - a risk assessment has been carried out
  - a method statement has been prepared
  - a permit to work system is in place.

☑ Other ways of doing the job must always be investigated before entry is made.

☑ Carrying out confined space working in an unsafe way has been the cause of many deaths, many by people who were trying to rescue other victims.

☑ If natural gas is detected in any occupied confined space (such as an underground service duct), it must be evacuated immediately.

☑ Forced-air mechanical ventilation must be provided where there is not enough breathable air.

☑ If oxyacetylene equipment is used in a confined space, the two main safety considerations are the following risks.
  - Unburnt oxygen causing an oxygen enriched atmosphere.
  - A flammable gas leak.

☑ Failure of the lighting in a confined space must be controlled by issuing workers with, as a minimum, torches.

☑ The use of hazardous substances, which can be breathed in, must be closely controlled in confined spaces.

F
24

Electrical safety

Electricity can be a killer. It cannot be detected by any of the senses except touch. Working close to live exposed equipment or circuits could result in a fatal shock. Here are some examples of good practice in electrical safety.

☑ Defective electrical equipment, including hand tools, must be taken out of service immediately and a procedure put in place to make sure they cannot be used.

☑ Extension leads must be run in a safe way so that they are not a tripping hazard. If possible run them above head height or along the join of the walls and the floor.

☑ Electrical distribution circuits must only be installed by competent and authorised electrical contractors.

☑ If the supply system does not meet your needs, tell someone and then stop work until an authorised supply has been installed.

☑ All mains (230 volt) and 110 volt equipment must be periodically tested for electrical safety, commonly known as 'PAT testing'.

☑ Battery-powered tools do not need PAT testing although any mains-powered battery chargers do.

☑ Temporary continuity bonding must be installed before breaking into metal pipework to provide a continuous earth for the installation throughout the duration of the work.

☑ Only battery-powered hand tools should be used to carry out work outside in wet weather.

☑ Testing for hidden cables within the structure of a wall should be carried out, using a cable tracer, before disturbing the fabric of the wall.

☑ Carry out the following before working on electrically powered equipment.
  - Make sure the equipment is switched off.
  - Isolate the supply at the main board.
  - Lock out and tag the circuit at the main supply board.
  - Test the circuit.

☑ If work has to be carried out on electrical equipment and the main isolator does not have a lock out device, the person(s) doing the job should carry out the following.
  - Withdraw and retain the fuses.
  - Display a clear warning sign on the isolator.

☑ If working near to live exposed conductors is unavoidable, a permit to work system must be put in place because most appliances and equipment run on mains voltage (230 volts).

☑ 110 volt power tools are used on site because they are safer; transformers are used to reduce the 230 volt supply to 110 volts.

☑ Electrical power equipment is often colour coded – 110 volt (yellow), 230 volt (blue) and 400 volt (red).

F
24

☑ When assembling a mobile tower scaffold, overhead electrical cables must be treated as live until it is confirmed that they are dead.

☑ No-one must start work near to exposed electrical conductors unless they are confirmed to be dead. Damaged cables must be isolated or replaced.

☑ The padlock to an electrical lock-out guard can be fitted by anyone working on the equipment.

☑ If the mains isolator for a piece of equipment is found switched off upon arrival on site, work must **not** start until the person in control of the premises has been consulted.

☑ There must be adequate task lighting, where there is not enough natural light to allow any job to be carried out safely.

Emergency situations

You may find that you are first on the scene following an accident to another worker, and it is important that you know what to do. Carry out the following if you find anyone who is injured.

☑ Make sure that you are not in any danger.

☑ Stay with the victim, keep them still and send someone else to find a first aider.

It is important that everyone on site knows what to do in an emergency situation. A serious emergency may result in the evacuation of the whole site.

☑ If a natural gas leak in an enclosed area is reported, the area should be ventilated and the gas emergency service should be contacted.

☑ The following steps must be taken if a refrigerant leak is reported in an enclosed area.
- The area must be ventilated.
- All naked flames must be extinguished.
- It must be established whether or not it is safe to enter the area before anyone tries to do so.

Health risks

Health risks are often overlooked because the symptoms are not often immediately obvious. Examples of health risks that may have to be managed are listed below.

☑ Asbestos is likely to be found in any building built before the year 2000.

☑ Anyone who is likely to disturb asbestos should be trained and training must be suitable for to the work being undertaken.

☑ Anyone who is likely to disturb the fabric of a building must be aware of the following.
- Asbestos could be present.
- Asbestos can be found in many places.
- Products include insulation boards around radiators, gaskets and seals in joints, and rope seals in a boiler.
- If the presence of asbestos is suspected, work must stop immediately and the situation must be reported to a supervisor or manager.

  Note: the asbestos register must be consulted before the work starts.

F
24

☑ Anyone suffering from headache or sickness whilst using a solvent-based product (such as adhesive) should be taken into fresh air. They will also need first-aid treatment.

☑ Discarded items of drug-using equipment must be safely removed by wearing gloves and using grips if practical. The supervisor or manager must be told.

☑ Manual handling must be carried out in a way that avoids injury.

  − Generally assessing the task as a whole before trying to lift items that are known to be heavy (such as rolls of lead).

  − Operatives telling their supervisor and asking for help if required to move any load that they know is too heavy for them to move without help.

  − Using a suitable manual handling aid, (such as a trolley) if needed, to move a heavy load, particularly over long distances.

☑ Repeatedly bending copper tube using an internal spring could result in long-term damage to the knees.

☑ Noise assessments must be carried out by a competent person where there is a danger of noise-induced hearing loss.

☑ When carrying out solvent welding on plastic ductwork it is essential that the area remains well ventilated.

☑ You can avoid risks to health from working with lead by carrying out the following.

  − Preventing it from getting into the bloodstream by washing your hands after handling it.

  − Not smoking whilst bossing or otherwise handling it.

☑ Potentially fatal risks from legionella can be controlled by being aware of the following.

  − The bacteria is spread to humans though breathing in water droplets in the form of fine mists and sprays.

  − Suitable respiratory protective equipment (RPE) with a protection factor of 40 must be worn when breaking into the system if exposure to sprays or mists cannot be prevented.

  − The ideal temperature range for the bacteria to breed is between 20°C and 45°C.

  − Breeding grounds for legionella include slow-moving or stationary water supplies (such as infrequently used shower heads or 'dead legs') that are within the above temperature range.

  − If an outbreak of legionella is suspected, the Health and Safety Executive must be informed immediately.

LPG and other gases

LPG is a flammable and explosive gas that is often found on construction sites. Many other bottled gases are dangerous if not handled and stored properly because they are explosive and are stored at high pressure. Some safety precautions are listed below.

☑ LPG cylinders that supply site cabins must be kept outside of the cabin.

☑ LPG and acetylene cylinders must be stored in the open air to prevent the build-up of leaking gas.

☑ If LPG bottles are transported and/or stored overnight in a van, there must be a low-level drainage route to the outside to protect against the accumulation of leaking LPG.

F
24

☑ Where LPG cylinders are being transported in a van they must be carried in a purpose-built container inside the vehicle and have an LPG sign on the outside of the vehicle.

☑ Anyone who has to transport more than 5 kg of LPG in a covered van must be trained and competent in the hazards relating to the gases.

☑ It is important to know the difference between equipment that is used on propane and butane because propane equipment works on a higher pressure.

☑ LPG is heavier than air and leaking gas will collect at the lowest point it can reach (such as basements, drains or gulleys). Avoid such features when using or storing LPG.

LPG store

☑ Except for cylinders designed for use on gas-powered forklift trucks, store all LPG cylinders in an upright position to prevent the liquid gas being drawn from the cylinder creating a hazardous situation.

☑ If a leak is suspected in any part of an LPG system efforts to trace it must only be made using a proper leak detection fluid.

☑ Oxygen cylinders must be handled with great care due to the high pressure to which they are filled.

☑ Ensure the following when using oxyacetylene equipment.
  – The bottles must be secured in an upright position.
  – The cylinders, hoses and flashback arrestors must be in good condition.
  – The area must be well ventilated and clear of any obstructions.
  – The bottles must be stored separate from other gas bottles in a special compound.
  – Green-tinted goggles manufactured to current standards must be worn by the person using the equipment.
  – It should not be used for jointing copper tube using capillary soldered fittings.
  – It should not be used for fitting capillary soldered fittings to copper tubing.

☑ Acetylene cylinders must also be stored away from other gases, outside in a special storage compound.

☑ It is important to be able to identify the content of gas cylinders by their colour. For this reason they are colour coded.
  – Propane cylinders are red or orange.
  – Acetylene cylinders are maroon.

☑ Where welding is being carried out, screens must be provided to protect others from welding flash.

Lifting operations

Lifting operations have been the cause of many accidents because they were not properly planned, carried out or defective equipment was used. Everyone involved in lifting operations must be aware of the following.

☑ The sequence of operations in any lifting activity must be laid out in advance in a method statement (sometimes called a lift plan).

☑ The safe working load (SWL) of any piece of lifting equipment or accessory must never be exceeded.

☑ Every piece of lifting equipment and each lifting accessory must be marked with their SWL.

☑ If any item of lifting equipment is found to be defective the equipment must not be used and the problem must be reported to a supervisor or manager.

☑ All items must be stable and secure whilst being lifted.

☑ Items that are lifted into a place where they will be installed must not be released from the hoist until securely fixed in place.

 All lifting equipment must be thoroughly examined periodically by a competent person.

Personal protective equipment

Wearing the correct personal protective equipment (PPE) can prevent exposure to harmful substances. The wrong type of PPE is likely to be useless. Always use the correct PPE (such as the items listed below), where a risk cannot be controlled by other measures.

☑ The correct type of impact and dust resistant eye protection when drilling, cutting or grinding any material that could produce flying debris.

☑ Thermally protective gloves to avoid direct skin contact with pipe-freezing equipment. Always read the COSHH assessment for the product.

☑ A safety helmet, protective footwear, hearing protection, suitable respiratory protective equipment (RPE) and eye protection when using a hammer drill.

☑ Ear defenders if working in a noisy environment or doing any job in which high levels of noise are produced.

☑ Green-tinted goggles if carrying out oxyacetylene welding.

☑ Safety gloves, suitable RPE, and eye protection if having to handle fibreglass roof insulation.

☑ Respiratory protective equipment (RPE) when using hazardous substances that can be breathed in. Do not start work if this hasn't been provided.

☑ Cut-resistant gloves when handling anything with sharp edges.

**F
24**

 Personal protective equipment should only be considered as a last resort.

Half face mask

Safety gloves

Safe methods of work

The importance of adopting safe methods of work, derived from carrying out a risk assessment and often given in a method statement, cannot be overstated. Some examples are shown below.

☑ The correct hand tools must be used for any job (such as using a hammer and bolster chisel for taking up floorboards).

☑ The transportation of tools and materials must be carried out in a safe and responsible way, examples are below.
  – Carrying long lengths of tubing in a pipe-rack attached to the roof of a van.
  – Fixing a ladder to the roof rack of a van using proper ladder-clamps.

☑ The exhaust fumes from vehicle exhausts are toxic; if engine-driven plant has to be run inside a building, the exhaust fumes must be extracted to a position outside the building.

☑ Liquid spills can be a slipping hazard, so tell your supervisor and keep people out of the area until they are cleaned up.

☑ Prevent contact with moving parts of machinery or rotating materials by enclosing them with guards or barriers.

☑ Be aware of sharp edges when using hand tools to cut through sheet material or pipes.

☑ Keep non-involved people out of the area when pressure testing pipework or vessels.

☑ Prevent the entanglement of clothing when using an electrically-powered threading machine.

☑ A permit to work system should be introduced for all high risk work activities.

☑ Before starting work on any piece of equipment it is essential that the operation and maintenance manual for the equipment is consulted.

☑ To prevent unauthorised access to plant and switchgear rooms the doors must always be kept locked.

☑ Where possible lone working should be avoided. A lone worker must register their presence with the site representative before starting work and a system of periodically checking on the lone worker must be in place.

F
24

Do not carry out tasks in an improvised way, using the wrong tool for the job.

Working at height

Examples of good practice for safe working at height are listed below.

☑ A risk assessment must have been carried out.

☑ If a ladder is used it should be secured to the structure against which it is resting to prevent it from slipping.

☑ When using a stepladder the restraining mechanism must be fully extended.

☑ Stepladders must only be used in the following situations.

  − If a risk assessment shows they are suitable for the job.

  − They are in good condition.

  − For light, short-term work (lasting no more than a few minutes) that does not involve stretching or reaching.

☑ When a mobile tower scaffold is used, generally only one working platform should be occupied at any one time.

Proprietary access system with ladder access, working platform, guard-rails and hoist

☑ When deciding the maximum height to which a mobile tower scaffold may be built the manufacturer's instructions must be referred to.

☑ The hatch of a mobile access tower working platform must be closed immediately after gaining access to the platform.

☑ Before moving a mobile tower, all people, tools and equipment must be removed from the working platform.

☑ The users of mobile tower scaffolds must be aware of the proximity of overhead live electric cables before erecting the tower.

☑ Edge protection must be fitted to working platforms to prevent the fall of a person or object, where this could result in injury or damage.

☑ A stable working platform (such as a mobile tower scaffold) should be used for jobs where there is a good floor surface and 'heavier' type work is to be carried out at height.

☑ If working near the edge of a flat roof that has a low parapet, edge protection consisting of double guard-rails and a toe-board must be installed at the roof edge.

☑ Ladders used on site must be labelled 'Class 1' (industrial). Any ladder labelled 'Class 2' or 'BS EN 131' (light trade) or 'Class 3' (domestic use only) must not be used.

☑ Wooden ladders that have been painted must not be used because the paint can hide defects.

F
24

☑ All shafts, pits, service ducts, large floor voids and so on, must be fitted with double guard-rails and toe-boards or a secure cover where someone could fall into them.

☑ If working at height to dismantle lengths of soil pipe, it can be safely carried out by working in pairs and breaking the length at the collar to remove complete sections.

☑ Flue liners must be installed in a safe way by working in pairs at roof level and using a safe method of access (such as a chimney scaffold).

☑ Falling objects must be prevented when working above occupied areas.

☑ As far as practical, access to ceiling voids or soffits containing a large number of services should be restricted. Other means of access may be needed.

☒ Never use services as a make-shift working platform or a means of access.

Domestic heating and plumbing services (HAPS)

Installing or maintaining heating and plumbing services can present the risk of injury or ill health. Some examples of good practice are listed below.

☑ Temporary continuity bonding should be carried out before removing and replacing sections of metallic pipework to provide a continuous earth for the pipework installation.

☑ When working where welding is being carried out, a screen should be provided to protect you from welding flash.

☑ The most likely risk of injury when cutting a pipe with hand-operated pipe cutters is because the inside edge of the cut pipe becomes sharp to touch.

☑ When transporting long lengths of pipe by van use a pipe rack fixed to the roof of the van. Ladder clamps should also be used to secure a ladder or stepladders to the roof rack of a van.

☑ When taking up a length of floorboard to install pipework you should use a hammer and bolster (and not a hammer with a chisel or screwdriver).

 If a job involves work below a ground-level suspended timber floor, you should first check or ask if the work could be performed from outside it, rather than entering a confined space.

Pipefitting and welding (industrial and commercial) (PFW)

Pipefitting and welding can present the risk of injury or ill health to you and others. Some examples of good practice are listed below.

☑ When using a pipe threading machine a safety barrier should be erected around the whole length of the pipe and you should make sure that your clothing cannot get caught on rotating parts of the machine.

☑ When a new piece of plant has been installed but has not been commissioned, it should be left with all valves and switches locked off.

F
24

☑ Before using oxyacetylene equipment it is essential to check the following.

- The cylinders, hoses and flashback arresters are in good condition.
- The area is well ventilated and clear of any obstructions.

☑ Acetylene cylinders (maroon in colour) should be stored outside in a special storage compound when not in use.

☑ When using oxyacetylene brazing equipment, the bottles should be stood upright and secured, preferably on a purpose made trolley.

☑ When using pipe-freezing equipment to isolate the damaged section of pipe, you should wear gloves to avoid direct contact with the skin and read the COSHH assessment.

Only those involved in carrying out the pressure testing of pipework or vessels should be present.

Ductwork (DUCT)

Installing or maintaining ductwork can present the risk of injury or ill health. Some examples of good practice are listed below.

☑ Before painting the external surface of any ductwork, you should read the COSHH assessment for the paint.

☑ Fume extraction must be provided when welding galvanised ductwork.

☑ Carry out the following after using a solvent based adhesive on ductwork.

- The ductwork must be left with the inspection covers off.
- 'No smoking' signs must be displayed.
- The area must be well ventilated.

☑ If, before fitting, a defect is noticed in any component of a system that is being installed, the item must not be fitted and you must tell your supervisor or manager.

☑ Before using a cleaning agent or biocide on a ductwork system:

- advice on the properties of the cleaning agent or biocide must be obtained from the manufacturer
- those doing the work must read the COSHH assessment for the cleaning agent or biocide
- an assessment of the risks of using the cleaning agent or biocide must be made
- a method statement for the work must be prepared
- the building occupier must be consulted.

☑ Before cleaning a system in an industrial laboratory or other premises where harmful particulates might be encountered:

- the system must be inspected
- samples must be collected from the system
- a job-specific risk assessment and method statement must be prepared.

F
24

☑ If it is necessary for a person to enter ductwork, two items that must be considered are the:
- dangers of working in confined spaces
- strength of the ductwork and its supports.

☑ Before working on a kitchen extraction system, the nature of the cooking deposits in the system should be established.

☑ Aluminium ductwork that has been pre-insulated with fibreglass must only be cut using tin snips, with the person doing the cutting wearing RPE suitable for protecting against airborne fibres.

☑ When jointing plastic-coated metal ductwork, welding presents far greater health risks than, for example, riveting, taping or using nuts and bolts.

 If dismantling waste-extract ductwork, it is essential to find out what it may be contaminated with before starting work.

Refrigeration and air conditioning (RAAC)

Refrigerants and other gases

Most gases have the potential to cause harm because they are explosive, stored at high pressure, are at low temperatures or are harmful to the environment. Examples of good practice and the unsafe properties of gases are shown below.

☑ When not is use, refrigerant cylinders must be stored in a special, locked storage compound in the open air.

☑ Refrigerant gases are heavier than air and if released into an enclosed space will sink to the lowest place they can seep into.

☑ If transported in a van, refrigerant bottles must be carried in a purpose-built container inside the vehicle.

☑ Flashback arrestors must be fitted between pipes and gauges of oxy-propane brazing equipment.

☑ When handling refrigerant gases, eye protection, overalls, thermal resistant gloves and safety boots must be worn.

☑ Ensure you check the following when pressure testing using nitrogen.
- The gauges can take the necessary pressure.
- The nitrogen bottle is secured in an upright position.

☒ Oxygen must never be used for pressure testing because it could react with the oil in the compressor causing an explosion possibly resulting in serious injury or death.

F
24

Safe methods of work

☑ Before entering a cold-room it must be established that the exit door is fitted with an internal handle.

☑ When a refrigerant leak has been reported in a closed area, it must be established that it is safe to enter before anyone tries to do so.

Services and facilities maintenance (SAF)

Checking, installing, testing and commissioning installations

Where new plant or equipment is being installed it must be done in a way that avoids injury to the people doing the job or anyone else. This must include ensuring that the plant or equipment cannot be operated in an unauthorised way before it has been commissioned and handed over.

☑ The health and safety file for any building, where one has been compiled, is a possible useful source of information on the safe way of maintaining the systems within it.

☑ In a normal office environment, the temperature of the hot water at the tap furthest from the boiler should be at least 50°C within one minute of starting to run it.

☑ The maximum temperature of a cold water supply must be 20°C within two minutes of starting to run it.

☑ The following are two examples of a pressure system.
  – Medium and high temperature hot water systems above 95°C.
  – Steam systems.

☑ A written scheme of examination must be in place before a pressure system is operated.

☑ Where there is a cooling tower on site, it must have a formal log book that is kept up to date.

☑ On cooling tower systems the water must be chemically treated.

☑ Make sure the following is carried out when replacing the filters in an air-conditioning system.
  – A job-specific risk assessment and method statement must be prepared and followed.
  – The person(s) doing the job must wear suitable overalls and a respirator.

☑ After a gas boiler has been serviced it must be checked for the following.
  – Flueing. – Gas rate.
  – Ventilation. – Safe functioning.

☑ Before adding an inhibitor to a heating system, the COSHH assessment for the product must be read and understood.

F
24

F
24

25

Plumbing (JIB)

What your site and employer should do for you

1. Provide you with a method of working that is safe and without risks to your health.

2. Ensure that a competent person supervises the work.

3. Inform you of the significant hazards identified in the risk assessment.

4. The safe way of working will be in a method statement which will be explained to you.

5. At no time place you in danger.

6. Provide you with adequate instruction and training.

What you should do for your site and employer

1. Follow the agreed safe system of work.

2. Not take risks with your own or anyone else's health or safety.

3. Report any aspect of your work which you feel is unsafe.

4. Comply with any permit systems which are in operation.

F
25

Introduction

Plumbing and gas-related work is highly specialised and potentially dangerous. All such work must be properly planned, only carried out by trained and competent contractors and adequately supervised as necessary.

No-one should attempt to work on any gas pipework or equipment unless they are a Gas Safe registered engineer.

 Poorly thought out or executed gas-related work activities can kill.

Safe methods of working

Safe working must include due attention to the following.

☑ Looking after equipment and hand tools to ensure they are safe to use, including carrying out simple repairs (such as replacing a split file handle) where this is practical.

☑ Being aware that cutting large diameter pipes will leave extremely sharp edges inside the pipe.

☑ Leaving all places of work in a safe condition if they have to be left unoccupied, particularly if working in domestic premises where the occupier will not be risk-aware.

☑ Ensuring safe access to any place of work and that the workplace itself is safe to occupy (for example using a ladder or stepladder if accessing the loft space of a domestic premises and ensuring that there is safe access over the joists).

☑ Carrying out the transportation of people, equipment and materials in a safe and responsible manner, examples are listed below.

   – Only carrying people in the back of a van if it is fitted with factory-fitted seats and seatbelts.

   – Carrying long lengths of tubing in a suitable pipe-rack attached to the roof of a van.

   – Always wearing a seat belt, when one is provided, if operating construction plant.

☑ If the sides of an excavation are not supported and show signs of collapse, it must not be entered by any person.

 Readers of this chapter should also refer to the 'Common elements' section of Chapter F24 Heating, ventilation, air conditioning and refrigeration (HVACR).

F
25

For further guidance refer to:

Joint Industry Board PMES England & Wales
Lovell House, Sandpiper Court
Phoenix Business Park
Eaton Socon
St Neots
Cambridge
PE19 8EP

Tel: 01480 476925

www.jib-pmes-org

F
25

Further information

Training record

Name of company

Name of employee

Name of supervisor

Instructions to supervisor

The employee and supervisor should sign each area of training listed below as it is completed and tick the box. The manager responsible should endorse the record and ensure that a copy is retained on file.

		Completed	Supervisor's signature
1	General responsibilities	☐	
2	Accident reporting and recording	☐	
3	Health and welfare	☐	
4	First aid and emergency procedures	☐	
5	Personal protective equipment	☐	
6	Asbestos	☐	
7	Dust and fumes (Respiratory hazards)	☐	
8	Noise and vibration	☐	

Supervisor's signature

Completed

9   Hazardous substances ☐

10 Manual handling ☐

11 Safety signs ☐

12 Fire prevention and control ☐

13 Electrical safety, tools and equipment ☐

14 Site transport safety ☐

15 Lifting operations ☐

16 Working at height ☐

17 Excavations and confined spaces ☐

18 Environmental awareness and waste control ☐

19 Demolition ☐

20 Highway works ☐

21 Specialist work at height ☐

22 Lifts and escalators ☐

23 Tunnelling ☐

24 Heating, ventilation, air conditioning and refrigeration (HVACR) ☐

25 Plumbing (JIB) ☐

I confirm that the named person has completed the training as listed:

Signed _____ **Date** _____

I confirm that I have received the training as listed: